Contents

Chapter 1   A Place to Belong   **1**

Part 1   Looking in the Mirror 15

Chapter 2   Blessing or Burden?   17
Chapter 3   The Basic Needs of People in Small Groups   **25**
Chapter 4   A Healthy Start   **37**
Chapter 5   Evaluate the Climate for Change   **47**
Chapter 6   The Dormant Church   **59**
Chapter 7   The Dedicated Church   **69**
Chapter 8   The Developing Church   **75**
Chapter 9   The Dynamic Church   **87**

Part 2   Two Effective Models 99

Chapter 10   The Slow Track Model   **101**
Chapter 11   The Fast Track Model   **107**

Part 3   Straight Talk on Small Groups 115

Chapter 12   Discovering Leaders   **117**
Chapter 13   The Sour Seven   **125**
Chapter 14   Organizing for Growth   **137**
Chapter 15   Developing Leaders   **147**
Chapter 16   The Life Cycles of Small Group Ministry   **163**
              Notes   **175**
              Bibliography for Further Study   **177**
              Resources for Further Study   **179**

93431

CREATING

COMMUNITY

CREATING
COMMUNITY

DEEPER FELLOWSHIP

THROUGH SMALL GROUP

MINISTRY

GLEN MARTIN & GARY MCINTOSH

BROADMAN
&HOLMAN
PUBLISHERS

Nashville, Tennessee

4261-00
0-8054-6100-0

Published by Broadman & Holman Publishers, Nashville, Tennessee
Acquisitions and Development Editor: John Landers
Page Design and Typography: TF Designs, Mt. Juliet, Tennessee

Dewey Decimal Classification: 259.8
Subject Heading: SMALL GROUP MINISTRIES
Library of Congress Card Catalog Number: 97-15829

Unless otherwise noted, Scripture quotations are from the Holy Bible, New International Version, © 1973, 1978, 1984 by International Bible Society. Other versions cited are KJV, the King James Version; NASB, the New American Standard Bible, © the Lockman Foundation, 1960, 1962, 1963, 1968, 1971, 1972, 1973, 1975, 1977, used by permission; NKJV, New King James Version, © 1979, 1980, 1982, Thomas Nelson, Inc., Publishers; and TLB, *The Living Bible,* © Tyndale House Publishers, Wheaton, Ill., 1971, used by permission.

Library of Congress Cataloging-in-Publication Data
Martin, Glen, 1953–
    Creating community : deeper fellowship through small
group ministry / Glen Martin, Gary McIntosh.
        p. cm.
    Includes bibliographical references.
    ISBN 0-8054-6100-0 (pbk.)
        1. Church group work. 2. Small groups—Religious aspects—Christianity. 3. Fellowship—Religious aspects—Christianity. I. McIntosh, Gary, 1947– . II. Title.
    BV652.2.M34   1997
    253'.7—dc21

                                                                    97-15829
                                                                    CIP

1 2 3 4 5 01 00 99 98 97

A Place to Belong

A lonely woman went to a pet store to purchase a parrot to keep her company. She took her new pet home but returned the next day to report, "That parrot hasn't said a word yet!"

"Does it have a mirror?" asked the storekeeper. "Parrots like to be able to look at themselves in the mirror." So the woman bought a mirror and returned home.

The next day she was back, announcing that the bird still wasn't speaking. "What about a ladder?" the storekeeper said. "Parrots enjoy walking up and down a ladder." So she bought a ladder and returned home.

Sure enough, the next day the woman was back with the same story—the parrot didn't talk. "Does the parrot have a swing? Birds enjoy relaxing on a swing," the storekeeper encouraged. In a final attempt to get her parrot to talk, she bought a swing and took it home.

The next day she returned to announce that the bird had died. "I'm terribly sorry to hear that," said the storekeeper. "Did the bird ever say anything before it died?"

"Yes," said the lady. "It said, 'Don't they sell any food down there?'"

Mirrors, ladders, and swings didn't meet the needs of the parrot in our story. Neither will they meet the needs of people in our churches. People are busy. They live in the fast lane and miss out on one of life's greatest ingredients: caring relationships. In our daily lives, we buy mirrors for primping, ladders for climbing to success, and swings for seeking pleasure and relief from stress. But where do we turn when we are lonely? Where can we go when we face a trial or temptation that seems beyond our personal level of tolerance? Where can we find the solace, rest, and love of a caring community? Small groups! That's where.

Whenever there was major persecution, God's people met in small home groups. Today we are not suffering persecution in the United States to the extent that Christians are being forced to meet in small home groups. However, many of our churches need renewal. Church growth researchers indicate that upwards of 85 percent of our churches either have plateaued or are declining. With approximately 400,000 Protestant churches in the United States, that means about 340,000 churches are candidates for some degree of spiritual renewal.

One common thread among spiritually healthy churches in the United States is the resurgence of small group ministry. Carl George, noted church growth researcher and consultant, wrote, "In short, the more caring cells your church has, the more people you can sustain and the more crisis you can handle without loss of quality. That means more people who will be able, in the name of Jesus Christ, to love a lost world and bring it to the Savior. Adequate caring lies at the foundation of all sound church growth."[1]

Moses on Ministry

The model of a "lone ranger" pastor who personally ministers to all the spiritual needs of a congregation fits many declining and plateaued congregations. Before the 1950s, that model of pastoral care fit the needs of churches. However, with the fracturing of families since midcentury, life has become so complex that no single pastor can personally care for every member of a congregation. As one pastor told us during a seminar coffee break, "I'm faced with codependency, divorce recovery, blended families, and all kinds of physical and emotional abuse issues in my ministry. Seminary didn't prepare me for this. I need some help!"

Often we get so caught up in what we are doing that we don't recognize that, by trying to handle everything ourselves, we are creating unnecessary problems. Sometimes we need the perspective of someone who is able to help us look at the situation from a different angle. There is an excellent example of this truth in Exodus 18.

Moses, of course, never started a small group ministry and never pastored a church. His concern revolved around the political and judicial needs of the people of Israel. However, in caring for the physical and spiritual needs of people, he faced complex issues that are similar to those we face today.

Following the nation of Israel's exodus from the land of Egypt, Moses found himself serving as the only judge for all the people. Whenever the people of Israel were in conflict, they came to Moses to ask his advice. Since he was the only judge, the people had to wait in long lines from early morning until late at night to have their complaints resolved. This resulted in high levels of stress for the people and Moses that are similar to those we face in churches today.

Moses Was at a Point of Burnout

Church leaders and pastors face this same reality. Burnout reveals itself in many ways. There are the physical characteristics, such as when a person lacks energy, maintains an exhausted appearance, and loses many of the normal desires that have always been a part of life. Then there are the emotional characteristics: a person becomes apathetic, loses all creativity, and cannot find any joy or satisfaction in what he or she is doing. And there are spiritual characteristics that may appear as moral letdowns, theological reversals, and shifting priorities.

Burnout has many causes. Stress, a natural ingredient of the ministry, causes burnout when it leads to prolonged distress and fatigue. Or burnout may be the result of conflicts. Wherever there is change, there is movement. Wherever there is movement, there is friction. When there is friction, there may be fracture. Much of a leader's time is spent trying to stop friction from becoming fracture. Prolonged conflict, however, can sap a person's energy and generate burnout.

Burnout can even be the result of prolonged high expectations. This was Moses' situation. Everyone had to have Moses' answer. Everyone needed to hear from the "top gun." These high expectations of people will inevitably cause the same burnout in any leader's life as it did in Moses'.

Dissatisfaction Was Increasing

Most of us have experienced the dissatisfaction of waiting for a doctor's appointment. Can you imagine the waiting line for Moses' attention and the dissatisfaction those people felt? Whenever there is a high level of dissatisfaction regarding leadership, there will be conflict. Generally speaking, pastors have a job that is ripe for role conflict and confusion. For instance, pastors structure their own time and have no regular supervision. They usually work alone and have trouble differentiating between work, family, recreation, and personal privacy. The most obvious problem is that people do not understand the true nature of a pastor's job. There is a list of unwritten expectations that forces pastors to perform a wide variety of job skills for which they may not be gifted. People wonder, *What does the pastor do all week?* Too often, we have found that there are few things that can be measured at the end of a pastor's day to signify accomplishments.

Historically, congregations rarely fired a pastor unless there was clear evidence of moral or ethical misconduct. People felt that they should not touch "the Lord's anointed" and, when dissatisfied with a pastor's performance, simply waited until he resigned. Lately it has become fairly common to hear of pastors being fired purely because people in the congregation are dissatisfied with the level of pastoral care. Small groups provide a way to meet the personal needs of people and raise the level of satisfaction.

The People Had an Unhealthy Dependence on One Person

An unhealthy church looks to only one person to meet everyone's needs. "No one else can solve my problem but you, Pastor" is a common statement. The healthy church motivates people to care for one another. Chuck Colson shared, "Contrary to popular impressions today, the pastor is not paid to do our work (service) for us. Pastors and teachers are to 'equip the saints'—that's us—to serve, to build the Body, to be the church in the world. Every lay person is to be equipped as a minister of the gospel."[2]

This shift in the understanding of pastoral care is pictured in figures 1 and 2. The first portrays an unhealthy dependence on one person for all pastoral care. The second portrays shared caring through a system of small groups.

Figure 1

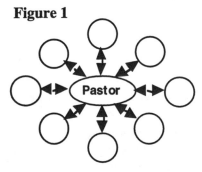

Figure 2

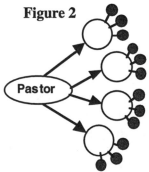

When Moses' father-in-law, Jethro, came for a visit, he handled the situation with much tact. He analyzed the current way of handling things from two perspectives. First, he reminded Moses that the people were being worn out. Second, he admonished him, "You cannot handle it alone."

Fortunately, Jethro had the wisdom not only to point out the problem but to offer a solution. He didn't attack Moses by saying, "Who do you think you are, trying to play God to all these people? You're not the only wise man in Israel. Get help!" No, instead he offered a well-thought-out plan. First, he acknowledged the importance of Moses' role in letting the people know the will of God. He suggested that Moses teach the people the decrees and laws of God to show them the right way to live and the duties they were to perform. Then he suggested that Moses train wise, honest men to be over units of people: thousands, hundreds, fifties, and tens. They could handle the less difficult cases and Moses would handle the tough ones. Next, Moses consulted God about the suggestions. Finally, Jethro pointed out the obvious. Moses' load would be lighter, enabling him to bear the burden because it would now be shared. In addition, the people would go home satisfied. Knowing the children of Israel, they were probably grumbling like mad! And not without cause. Moses listened to Jethro and did everything he said. Capable men from throughout Israel were appointed as leaders of the people. There were officials over thousands, hundreds, fifties, and tens. They judged the people at all times, bringing only the difficult cases to Moses.

What a great illustration of a win-win situation. Jethro won by presenting a great solution to his son-in-law's problem. The people won by getting satisfaction for their problems much faster. Moses won by expanding his leadership base and sharing his workload with others. The leaders won by being significantly used by God in accomplishing His purposes in ministry. They undoubtedly received the blessings that come to those who serve the Lord. Certainly this must have been a significant turning point in Moses' ministry as he allowed others to play an integral part in what the Lord was doing.

Seven Reasons Churches Need Small Groups

The caring and supportive environment of small groups is based on the concept of community. "Real community is people. Not just where they meet, when they meet, the experiences they have or have not had. Community in the local church has to do with how people relate, listen, confront, stimulate, forgive, tell the truth, pray and protect."[3]

Robert Banks suggests that in the early church world and culture, "Traditionally there had been two main types of community with which people might associate themselves: *politeia,* the public life of the city or nation state to which people belonged; and *oikonomia,* the household order into which they were born or to which they were attached."[4] The actual term *community* is more of an expression of the Spirit at work in the lives of a group of people than it is just a gathering together or assembly. It is the kind of community in which we are called brothers and sisters, fellow workers and slaves, and the *ekklesia,* or called-out ones, in the New Testament. This is what people are looking for today, a community where they can know and be known. A place to love and be loved. A relationship in which they can care and be cared for.

There are seven key reasons why churches need to initiate a small group ministry that will generate the kind of community that was seen in the early church.

Reason 1: Small Groups Encourage Spiritual Growth

Acts 2:42 reads, "They devoted themselves to the apostles' teaching and to the fellowship, to the breaking of bread and to prayer." The call of the church has never changed—"make disciples."[5] The process of making disciples can be broken down into three facets: evangelism, assimilation, and education. The foundation for discipleship is the Word of God and prayer. Community Baptist Church in California has identified the importance of community in the flow of this process as shown in figure 3.

Figure 3

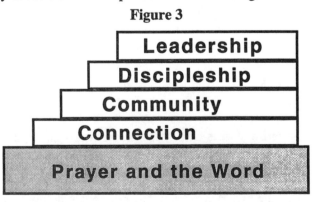

Building on the foundation of prayer and the Word of God, the first step is *connection*, when there is an attempt to get people into the church whether the primary means be direct mail, friendship evangelism, or special events. Then comes *community*, when this particular church is getting 75 percent of the newcomers into a place where they can grow spiritually—small groups. The last two steps, *discipleship* and *leadership*, naturally take place in the community of small groups. Remember, Christ's call to the church was to make disciples, not converts.

Reason 2: Small Groups Nourish Relational Growth

We all need to be loved. Yet, finding and sustaining close relationships can be one of life's most difficult experiences. God has created us with a deep-seated need for fellowship. Fellowship is more than just red punch and cookies after a church potluck.

Fellowship is being part of God's family and spending time with the other children. Hebrews 10:25: "Let us not give up meeting together, as some are in the habit of doing, but let us encourage one another—and all the more as you see the Day approaching."

Fellowship is the encouragement of other believers to grow spiritually. "And let us consider how we may spur one another on toward love and good deeds" (Heb. 10:24). Scripture also reminds us that growth happens when we rub shoulders with one another. "As iron sharpens iron, so one man sharpens another" (Prov. 27:17).

Fellowship is the power of God when we gather together. We must remember that Jesus said, "For where two or three come together in my name, there I am with them" (Matt. 18:20). The power is revealed in Matthew 18:19, "Again, I tell you that if two of you on earth agree about anything you ask for, it will be done for you by my Father in heaven." There is power when the people of God gather together to pray.

Fellowship presents a picture of Christ to a lost world. Our Lord's great high priestly prayer in John 17 revealed His heart and desire for the church. "My prayer is not for them alone. I pray also for those who will believe in me through their message, that all of them may be one, Father, just as you are in me and I am in you. May they also be in us so that the world may believe that you have sent me" (vv. 20–21). We demonstrate the reality of Jesus Christ in our lives by the love we have for one another.

Reason 3: Small Groups Build Emotional Support

Anxiety and stress have become a natural part of life as people pursue the American dream. We think that a couple of tablespoons of Pepto-Bismol and a few hours sleep will make us fine. But this is not proving to be true. Add to this the fact that there are many who are living alone, and you have all the ingredients for breakdowns in the midst of crisis. "Today, one in four Americans live alone, but the number of new, one-person households is growing rapidly. Once viewed as the unfortunate fate of lonely bachelors and spinsters, living alone gained popularity during the 1960s and '70s as young people put off marriage and the elderly used their increasing financial resources to buy independence from relatives."[6]

This aloneness is not altogether good. Modern trends of depression and inability to cope with rising pressures have sparked an increase in suicides. "Unfortunately, research studies show that 15% of people with severe clinical depression will die of suicide." Depression affects every age group. According to the National Mental Health Association, more than eleven million Americans suffer from clinical depression each year, and suicide is "now the second leading cause of death among people between the ages of 15 and 24."[7] What often causes depression is living in the gap between what we have and what we want, where we are and where we want to be.

Small groups provide a natural and nurturing setting for support and encouragement. They allow people to be themselves, admit their weaknesses without fear of rejection or retaliation, and promote healing as people are able to admit they have problems.

Reason 4: Small Groups Stimulate Service

As members of God's family, we have a responsibility to every other member of God's family. First Peter 4:10 revealed, "Each one should use whatever gift he has received to serve others, faithfully administering God's grace in its various forms." Our gifts are not for ourselves. They are for the entire body. Whenever even one of those gifts is not being used, then the body is not functioning at its very best. Small groups provide an excellent place for someone with the gift of hospitality to open up his or her home for meetings and meals. Another, whose gift is administration, could be responsible for attendance and follow-up. Those with the gifts of encouragement and mercy may want to set up the social functions and make sure that everyone is included.

This service can grow beyond the group as well. One church has a group of men who call themselves "The Gray Tigers." Their input into the body is to work at their church six to eight hours each week, fixing the little things that get broken and praying for the staff. The list is endless. But the important thing to remember is that we are to serve the rest of the body in response to God's love and working in our lives personally.

Reason 5: Small Groups Help Incorporate Newcomers

Small groups are the ideal environment for assimilation. In our book *Finding Them, Keeping Them*,[8] we suggest that three primary factors must be a part of the life of a newcomer in order to ensure that he or she will want to stay in a church. The factors are friendships, a ministry, and a small group. What is the ideal place for friendships to develop and grow? Where can new people sense that they are needed when most of the congregation does not know them yet? That's right . . . small groups. But small groups soon become saturated. If we plan on reaching more people for Christ, we must continually add new small groups.

Small groups, like any other assembly of people, can become saturated in two ways. First, they can suffer from *facility saturation:* the room fills up and there is no more room for anyone else to fit into the room or home. This normally occurs when the facility is 80 percent full. Second, small groups can suffer from *fellowship saturation:* the people have been together for some time (usually at least eighteen to twenty-four months), and new people find it difficult to move into their sphere of friendships. The solution to both facility saturation and fellowship saturation is to begin new groups.

Reason 6: Small Groups Develop Leadership

There are three main requirements for an effective church: leadership, leadership, leadership. Leadership is more caught than taught. It is often discovered rather than developed. Our Lord modeled effective leadership in a small group of twelve men. If modeling is to be effective, several ingredients must come into play:

- Frequent contact with the model
- A relationship that allows for exposure and vulnerability
- Variety of life settings

- Demonstration of beliefs and standards
- Examples along with instructions

The nonthreatening environment of a small group is the ideal setting for such modeling to take place.

Reason 7: Small Groups Help Sustain the Great Commission Focus

Many churches find it easy to plateau or begin declining when their church building is full. Our culture is very facilities-oriented and has difficulty seeing beyond the walls of the campus. Often the vision for continued growth is lost because of the facilities.

Small groups keep the church focused on the Great Commission. Every person should be involved in fulfilling the Great Commission. Why?

Great Commission vision requires us to obey Christ. The Lord gave us the Great Commission, and it is found throughout the New Testament.

"Therefore go and make disciples of all nations, baptizing them in the name of the Father and of the Son and of the Holy Spirit, and teaching them to obey everything I have commanded you. And surely I am with you always, to the very end of the age." (Matt. 28:19–20)

He said to them, "Go into all the world and preach the good news to all creation." (Mark 16:15)

And repentance and forgiveness of sins will be preached in his name to all nations, beginning at Jerusalem. (Luke 24:47)

Again Jesus said, "Peace be with you! As the Father has sent me, I am sending you." (John 20:21)

"But you will receive power when the Holy Spirit comes on you; and you will be my witnesses in Jerusalem, and in all Judea and Samaria, and to the ends of the earth." (Acts 1:8)

How, then, can they call on the one they have not believed in? And how can they believe in the one of whom they have not heard? And how can they hear without someone preaching to them? And how can they preach unless they are sent? As it is written, "How beautiful are the feet of those who bring good news!" (Rom. 10:14–15)

The Great Commission is the heartbeat of the church, and anything less than full obedience in every area of ministry is disobedience. It means we are either procrastinating and delaying our responsibility because of personal comfort and desires or we do not fully understand the instruction of Christ.

Great Commission vision requires us to show God's love. God's total love was demonstrated by Jesus' total surrender. Everything that our Savior has ever done or continues to do for us—His incarnation, suffering, death, resurrection, intercession, and glorification—He does because He loves us. If we fail to love like Christ and just perform our Christian duty, we are no more than a "clanging symbol" in a world that's got enough disjointed noises already (see 1 Cor. 13).

Not long after he had denied the Lord three times, Jesus came to Peter, who was busy at the nets once again, and confronted him to restore fellowship. His question to Peter: "Simon son of John, do you truly love me more than these?" (John 21:15b). That remains a crucial question to be answered by each of us individually. Small group ministry is a prime way to actively give and accept the love of God from each other.

Great Commission vision gives us a sense of fulfillment in life. God desires success in each one of our lives. Joshua 1:8 tells us, "This book of the law shall not depart from your mouth, but you shall meditate on it day and night, so that you may be careful to do according to all that is written in it; for then you will make your way prosperous, and then you will have success" (NASB). We must remember that success must be determined through God's eyes, not the world's eyes. That's why this passage begins with a call to be in the Scriptures so that we will know what is successful to God. Success in life is understanding God's life purpose for us and following it. Success is discovering how God has gifted us and responding to His call to serve the body of Christ, His church. And success is found in bearing fruit. Seeing another person come to Christ is one of the greatest experiences offered in our lives. Sadly many Christians lack fulfillment and demonstrate a life of depression and frustration because they fail to maintain a right relationship with Christ or they fail to share His love with the people around them. A small group is a place to learn of God and to safely bring these aspects of life into clearer focus.

Why Another Book on Small Groups?

In the 1950s and 1960s there were very few books available on the topic of small groups. Most churches emphasized the Sunday school which, for most people, met their needs of fellowship and community quite well. The strong economy of the fifties and sixties allowed churches to purchase land and construct educational buildings at reasonable costs. As Sunday school classes filled, new classrooms were constructed to make room for additional classes. However, as the economy began to slow in the 1970s and 1980s, land became more expensive, and the construction of new facilities faced new obstacles. Without the easy access to new classrooms, expanding Sunday school classes to meet the needs of fellowship and care became more difficult. The need for less costly meeting places along with the diversification of personal problems created interest in small groups once again. Today, if you look at the shelves of your local Christian bookstore, you will discover a large number of books available on this topic. So why write another book on small group ministry?

We have been personally involved with small groups in local churches for more than thirty years. As a pastor, Gary started a small group ministry in a church that averaged 125 worshipers on Sunday mornings. He understands the unique demands of overseeing a small group ministry in a church that is struggling to simply provide a basic ministry. Glen's leadership of a church of fourteen hundred worshipers involved the installation of a small group ministry as a means to provide pastoral care for a large congregation. He understands the issues involved in the larger church context. Both of us have led national seminars and advised churches on how to start, manage, and expand small groups.

As we've traveled, consulting with churches and leading small group seminars, we've noticed that not all churches have the *will* and *skill* to begin an effective small group ministry. While there are quite a number of fine books on the topic of small group ministry, *Creating Community* uniquely offers ideas for evaluating the readiness of a church to begin a small group ministry. Part 1 will assist you in evaluating your church's will and skill to start and successfully run a small group ministry. The evaluation tool found in chapter 5 will categorize your church as one of four types: The Dormant Church, The Dedicated Church, The Developing Church, or The Dynamic Church. Based on which category your church falls into, part 2 will then suggest two models for implementing small groups in your church. We then offer some straight talk about leadership skills that are necessary for the continued growth and development of your small group ministry in part 3.

If you are just beginning to study the possibility of using small groups in your church, we suggest you read the entire book. However, if you are already convinced of your need to get started, you may go directly to chapter 5 to evaluate your readiness and proceed to the chapter that speaks to the category your church falls into. *Creating Community* will help you to design an effective small group ministry that is right for your church in whatever category it falls.

Many years ago at the University of Wisconsin there was an undergraduate literary club that consisted of male students who had demonstrated outstanding talent in writing. At each meeting one of the students would read aloud a story or essay he had written and then submit it to the others for criticism. The criticism was brutal. Nothing was held back. The students showed no mercy in dissecting the material line by line. So hateful were the sessions that the members called themselves "The Stranglers."

Then a similar club was formed. It was called "The Wranglers." The Wranglers were female students with outstanding writing ability. Like their male counterparts they would read their writings at meetings and would critique one another. There was one noticeable difference. The Wranglers' criticism was gentle, thoughtful, positive, and kind. They lifted each other up and encouraged one another.

Twenty years later, a university researcher looked at the careers of the members of both groups. Not one of the bright young talents in the Stranglers had achieved a literary reputation of any kind. The Wranglers, on the other hand, had produced a half dozen prominent, successful writers. What was the difference? The formats of both groups were similar. Both groups had very talented students. The difference was that the Stranglers cut each other down while the Wranglers lifted each other up. The Stranglers strangled the life out of one another. The Wranglers enhanced each others' lives.[9]

The church in Acts was filled with Wranglers. Wouldn't it be great to recapture the enthusiasm and energy of that early church? Wouldn't it be great to have that same kind of love and harmony? How was it that those in the early church were Wranglers and not Stranglers? There was a sense of genuine, caring relationships among those who attended the early church, the kind of relationships that people are searching for today. This is what small groups have to offer your church. As you evaluate your church's readiness for small groups and gain insights into how to start a small group ministry, you will be on the way to creating community in your own church.

PART ONE

Looking in the Mirror

CHAPTER TWO

Blessing or Burden?

"It all started long before I came," said the Reverend Jason Kirk. And he was correct. Rev. Kirk is a fictional pastor, in a parable by Thomas H. Troeger, who was pastoring Clyde's Corner Church. The founder of this particular church, Cedric Clyde, was a successful farmer at the turn of the century. To demonstrate his love for God and his devotion to God's work, he paid for the building of this local church. Just before Cedric died, he donated furniture for the church's parlor and one item for the raised chancel behind the pulpit: "a giant red horsehair couch whose rich color Cedric fancied would brighten the front of the church." The huge chair featured massive curved arms and dark mahogany legs, each carved like the claw of a lion.

Time passed, and that couch became the subject of a bitter debate between members of the Clyde family, who wanted to keep it where it was, and newer members, who thought the couch did not belong in the sanctuary. This debate sparked tension between the established members and the newer families, who had moved to the country to get their children away from the drugs that were spreading into their suburban neighborhoods. These newer families had bought up foreclosed farms and built beautiful homes in the hills. They were accustomed to fine furnishings and detested what they had dubbed "the Victorian Leviathan" that dominated what otherwise was a plain but handsome church.

The Clyde family viewed the couch in a different light. Their farms had fallen on hard times in recent years. They looked at the couch each Sunday and fondly remembered that their great-grandfather Cedric had founded the church. Although their tractors may have been rusting in the front yard, at least the preacher sat on Cedric's couch.

"Every sentence I put in the air," Rev. Kirk remarked of his sermons, "I see them all weighing whether it is ammunition for their side or the other side. Here I am preaching about the love of God, and everything I say is filtered through a single question: Is the pastor in favor of the red horsehair couch, or is the pastor against the red horsehair couch?"[1]

This story is fictitious, but it is true to life. Many church leaders face problems like this. It may not be a red couch that is dividing your church, but it may be the debate over which translation of the Bible to use, a discussion about which kind of building should be next on the agenda, the decision on which music to choose for the upcoming Christmas program (traditional or contemporary), or whether small groups will be a burden or a blessing to the church. A healthy, vibrant church cannot function by maximizing its differences and minimizing cooperation.

The apostle Paul knew about such divisiveness. Just read his letters, and you will discover Paul's major concern for unity in the body of Christ. One aspect of biblical unity is found in a church's desire to build a sense of community within the church family.

The Call of the Church

After the Los Angeles riots, Steve Futterman of CBC radio broadcast an interview he had with one of the riot's many looters. The man had been one of many people who had looted a record store. When asked what he had stolen, the man replied, "Gospel tapes. I love Jesus."[2]

Unfortunately this is all too often the portrayal of Christians that the world sees. Yet Jesus defined His followers as the "salt of the earth." Jesus never told them that one day they would become the salt of the earth, but that they were already the salt of the earth. Salt would have been a valuable commodity in the culture of these disciples to whom Jesus was speaking. Salt was the primary means for preserving food before refrigeration was available. Salt was also an antiseptic that was vital to the cleaning of wounds and fighting infection. The most important quality of salt is that it never loses its taste. Salt will always be salt in its purest form. Jesus was telling His disciples, and us today, that once people become followers of Jesus, there is no turning back. In light of this conviction, God has placed the church on earth for several reasons.

The Church Is a Place of Redemption

The true church is a place where the unbeliever can come to hear how to be in a right relationship with God. Too frequently the church has lost this message and has become only a place for fellowship, even a place to find new clients for an insurance business. Fellowship is important, but without salvation—without a redeemed life—the church becomes nothing more than a social club. Too many churches today have "lost their savor" by allowing themselves to be contaminated by the world's ways. They have lost their God-given direction and purpose. God designed the church to be light to those living in darkness, to be salt to those who are perishing. The church must keep its priorities in place if it is to be all that God intends it to be.

The Church Is to Equip Christians

Paul wrote to the church in Ephesus, "It was he [Jesus Christ] who gave some to be apostles, some to be prophets, some to be evangelists, and some to be pastors and teachers, to prepare God's people for works of service, so that the body of Christ may be built up until we all reach unity in the faith and in the knowledge of the Son of God and become mature, attaining to the whole measure of the fullness of Christ" (Eph. 4:11–13).

The Church Is a Place for Fellowship

Yes, fellowship is important. The church can provide a wonderful setting for believers to meet together, to enjoy the company of people of like mind, and to learn from each other. The writer of Hebrews warns us to "not give up meeting together" (Heb. 10:25). There is a good reason for that. We are more vulnerable to enemy attacks if we are in our battle alone. Also, being together helps us keep a healthy perspective. We can be salt and light to each other as we encourage one another from our own experiences and pray for the needs of other believers. It is harder for the enemy to attack those who are in a healthy, supporting group. The loner becomes easy prey for enemy attacks.

Worth the Investment?

Small groups are a blessing when they are a place for redemption, for equipping, and for community. However, some churches harbor a continuing fear that small groups may become a burden.

Pastor Thomas sat at his desk, staring at the article he had just read, "Building a Successful Men's Ministry." The article was inspiring and challenging, and for a moment he caught a vision of what such a ministry might do in his church. But the more he thought about it, the more he felt restless and uncomfortable. He knew his church needed such a ministry, but in the three years he had been its pastor, there had been so many struggles in getting to the current place of stability that he shuddered to think of doing anything that might stir the waters and rock the boat. Questions and doubts flooded his mind.

True, the church is not accomplishing all it can, but why risk initiating something that will take a lot of my time and might cause more trouble than good? And what if Jim Tanner tries to take control? I remember how he tried to challenge me last time. He has given me enough grief already. I really don't want to create an opportunity for him to weaken my authority here. No, I think I'll pass on this one for now. Maybe later, when I feel more capable of handling the possible negatives, I'll start one. But for now I've got more than enough on my plate.

Why do we fear? Fear is not from God. We do not want to fear. It is not manly to fear, and yet we fear. Fear that keeps us from starting new things can be traced back to the Fall. It is the result of our fallen nature. It has subtle roots in not fully trusting God, in looking at the past, dreading the future, in wanting to do things our own way—and our own way in this instance is not to risk. This area of risk encompasses change. And change involves the unknown. Just thinking of the "what ifs" can paralyze the strongest of men if his eyes focus on the uncertainties of the future and not on God.

That is why change is always difficult. It is human nature to want the status quo, even though we may not like all it involves. Our emotions buy into the idea that it is better to stay with the problems we know than to risk change to get the possible good we don't know. In fact, many of the things that run through our mind when we experience fear are simply lies that the Enemy of our soul uses as strongholds to keep us from doing God's will.

Seven Fears

We have identified seven common fears of leaders who consider starting a small group ministry. The Enemy targets these leaders with many lies, hoping they will buy the lies and not do what God wants. As we look at each fear, we will note the lies that we may be buying into. Then we will look at the truth from God's perspective. Finally, we will see biblical principles, examples, and verses that counter these lies and can help us see the truth and resist each fear.

1. Fear of Change

The Dilemma. The unknown is often intimidating. We know what is happening now. What may our church look like if we change?

The Lies. "Change is not desirable." "Changes are risky." "Why should you try something new? Things are working fairly well now." "People will criticize us if we try this."

The Right Perspective. If God is showing you to do this, He will make the change work out for the best. Growth requires change.

Biblical Example/Principles. Peter resisted eating unclean food or associating with Gentiles in the presence of Jewish believers.

2. Fear of Failure

The Dilemma. There is always risk when we step out into something new. Success is never guaranteed from the world's perspective. Pride is a factor here—wanting to succeed and not be seen as weak or incapable. This is why some people will attempt only to do things they know they can succeed at.

The Lies. "There is too much to risk. You may fail if you try something new." "There are too many unknowns." "You're going to get in trouble if you try this and it doesn't work."

The Right Perspective. God does not lead us into failure. Just be certain He is leading you this way, and you will succeed as you follow His guidance.

Biblical Example/Principles. Moses didn't want to be the spokesperson to the Israelites. David modeled the opposite attitude. Everything looked like he should fail against Goliath, but he knew what God wanted and therefore trusted Him to use him to succeed. Psalm 1:3 says of the man who walks in God's ways, "Whatever he does prospers."

3. Fear of Inadequacy

The Dilemma. Insecurity has been part of the human makeup since the Fall. No one feels completely capable, especially when trying something new.

The Lies. "You can't pull it off. You've never tried this before." "What makes you think you can make this happen?" "This is not your area of strength." "You're not ready to try this. You don't know enough."

The Right Perspective. God is asking you to do this. Therefore He knows you can with His help. When you succeed, you will know that it was not you who did it because of your "capability," but He, and He will get all the glory, not you. Also, He can and will bring others alongside of you to help you make this endeavor successful.

Biblical Example/Principles. "I can do all things through Christ who strengthens me" (Phil. 4:13 NKJV). Paul said, "When I am weak, then I am strong" (2 Cor. 12:10). "But whoever listens to me will live in safety and be at ease, without fear of harm" (Prov. 1:33b).

4. Fear of Criticism

The Dilemma. We all want to be appreciated for our work. We want to please others and are fearful of what they might say. Yet most leaders are criticized. Criticism is a form of rejection and therefore is painful. Thus, it is natural to want to avoid any more opportunities for people to criticize us. Pride again comes in—wanting to be right, to be liked, and accepted.

The Lies. "We've never had one before. Why now?" "You don't understand our needs. This is wrong." "It won't work!" "No one will be interested or have enough time." "This is just another thing to waste our time and take time away from our families." "We already offer enough for everyone."

The Right Perspective. Satan is the accuser of the brethren. To not do something we know God wants, simply because we might get criticized, is to let the Enemy win. Let God fight your fights. Let Him be responsible for your reputation.

Biblical Example/Principles. Most biblical leaders including Moses, David, Nehemiah, Jesus, and Paul had their critics, but they listened only to what the Lord wanted them to do. God promised to be the One who gives us honor and to exalt our names, our reputations: "Through my name his horn will be exalted"; "His horn will be lifted high in honor" (Ps. 89:24; 112:9b).

5. Fear of Others

The Dilemma. No one likes conflict. We tend to avoid those things we know might cause it, especially with people who have influence. When there are power struggles in the church that involve you, fear may keep you from stepping out to do something new. People have been wanting you to do other things that you have turned down for lack of time; what will it look like if you now start this project? Will they feel slighted or hurt?

The Lies. "I will look bad if I try and fail. If I fail, then _____[names] will be able to undermine me more with others." " _____[names] will never agree. They will fight me on this." "I don't want to give _____[names] any more ammunition to use against me. It's hard enough as it is!"

The Right Perspective. We must be more concerned with what God thinks than with what man thinks. Remember, when we allow anyone to keep us from doing what we know is God's will, we are sinning. That person becomes more important to us than God. Leave the responses of others in God's hands.

Biblical Example/Principles. Let God fight your battles. "The fear of the LORD is the beginning of knowledge" (Prov. 1:7b). "The fear of the LORD leads to life: Then one rests content, untouched by trouble" (Prov. 19:23). Joshua told his men after they were victorious over their enemies and had their feet on the necks of their enemy, "Do not be afraid; do not be discouraged. Be strong and courageous. This is what the LORD will do to all the enemies you are going to fight" (Josh. 10:25). "On the contrary, we speak as men approved by God to be entrusted with the gospel. We are not trying to please men but God, who tests our hearts" (1 Thess. 2:4). "Whatever you do, work at it with all your heart as working for the Lord, not for men" (Col. 3:23). "What, then, shall we say in response to this? If God is for us, who can be against us?" (Rom. 8:31).

6. Fear of Lack of Time

The Dilemma. Taking on another project will inevitably take time. You probably already feel stretched to the breaking point. Your family may be complaining that you are always gone or always doing something at church. Your stress level may be high right now because of time constraints.

The Lies. "There is nothing that will come from this that will free up time for me. This will only take time away from my family." "I don't have enough time as it is." "I just can't add another thing." "If I add this, something else will suffer."

The Right Perspective. (1) God is a good God who is all-knowing and wants the very best for you. He has asked you to start a new ministry. Trust

Him. He knows your time problems. He does not want to overload you. He wants the best for you and the ministry. (2) It may be that developing a new ministry will help you free up more time as you develop leaders to whom you can delegate things you are now doing. (3) View the start-up time of this ministry to be like the teacher's time invested in training an assistant who will eventually share some of the workload.

Biblical Example/Principles. Jesus had a ministry with groups of 120, 70, and 12 people. He needed them to be trained so at the right time they could go out to minister and multiply His impact on the world. In addition, His ministry was a better one because He had people whom He was developing. He chose not to minister in a vacuum. In so doing, He set the example for our ministries today. The apostles delegated to others so they could have more time for their priorities. It took trained people to free them up (see Acts 6:1–6). "But I trust in you, O LORD; I say, 'You are my God.' My times are in your hands" (Ps. 31:14–15b).

7. Fear of the Past

The Dilemma. We wrongly look at the past as the blueprint for the future. Even if we were not in leadership when something was unsuccessfully tried, its failure can keep us from trying as others warn us of the futility of trying it again. Or we may have tried it in another setting that was less than successful and feel gun-shy to try it in a different setting.

The Lies. "We've never done this before." "We tried this twice, and it didn't work." "If it hasn't worked in the past, it won't work now." "Don't risk trying something that has had problems before."

The Right Perspective. (1) If God is leading us to do this now, the events of the past have no significance for today. (2) We are a different leadership, congregation, and even society than when we tried and failed in the past.

Biblical Example/Principles. We are told to forget the past in Philippians 3:13. Peter had to deal with his past failures in order to be able to lead the church. Judas did not deal with his past when he became Jesus' disciple, and as a result he failed the Lord.

What fears are you facing in your church as you consider starting a small group ministry? It is time to face your fears and take to heart the words of Paul to Timothy, "For God hath not given us the spirit of fear; but of power, and of love, and of a sound mind" (2 Tim 1:7, KJV).

CHAPTER THREE

The Basic Needs of People in Small Groups

An old Jewish story tells of a rabbi who asked the Lord to show him heaven and hell. "I will show you hell," said the Lord as He opened the door to a room. Inside was a large round table with a pot of delicious stew in the center. The people in the room were equipped with long-handled spoons, but they were starving. They were able to dip into the stew quite easily, but because the spoon handles were longer than a person's arm, they were unable to get the nourishing food to their mouth.

"Now I will show you heaven," said the Lord. This time the rabbi saw a room identical to the first, except that the people were well nourished, laughing, and talking. They had the same long-handled spoons, but somehow had overcome this handicap. To the puzzled rabbi, the Lord explained, "It's simple, but requires a certain skill—they have learned to feed each other."

The people in heaven were obviously prospering in an atmosphere of giving and receiving. If someone refused to give and receive, the system would collapse. This story clearly illustrates a central need for members of any small group: each needs to be willing to give and receive. However, other needs exist that should be understood and addressed if a group wants the loyalty, interest, and best efforts of its members.

A Sense of Belonging

People want to be wanted. They need to have confidence in their small group and its leadership based on the assurance of consistent, fair treatment and recognition when it is due.

The world we live in is marked by loneliness. Certain sociological conditions have become the enemy of natural community and have made it necessary for us to place an intentional emphasis on building Christian community. Note the following sociological changes in our society that, for many, lead to feelings of loneliness.

The Changing Family

The move from the extended family (in which multiple generations lived together) to the nuclear family (the immediate family of father, mother, and children) to the fractured family (single-parent and blended families) seems to be leading our society on an increasing course toward aloneness.

The Disappearance of Neighborhoods

Neighborhoods are places where people know and care for each other. In new housing tracts today the first things to go up are privacy fences. People don't want to be involved with their neighbors; they want the privilege of privacy to do their own thing.

The Fragmentation of Our Lives

It used to be that people knew each other in numerous spheres of their lives. A person with whom you worked was also in your church and social circle. There were multiple levels of interaction with the same people. Today we live fragmented lives in which we know people only in a single sphere. Often there is a different set of ethics and norms for each different sphere. We do not wholly know each other. Rather, we only have a fragmentary acquaintance, which leads to feelings of isolation and loneliness.

Figure 4

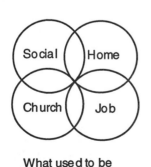

What used to be · What is today

The Mobility of Our Society

Long-term relationships are fewer and fewer as approximately one in every five American families moves every year. Highly mobile people tend to make friends fast but do not make long-lasting ones. The depth of care and sharing is often shallow in quick friendships; it takes knowing someone for a period of time before enough comfort develops to share deeply. The church, of course, depends on long-lasting relationships.

The Urbanization of Our Society

The move of our society to the city and suburbs has caused us to be less friendly, simply because we cannot relate to so many people. It is a paradox that one can live in New York or Los Angeles with literally millions of people and yet feel extremely lonely. Such is our world today even in small cities and communities.

The Spectator Culture

People who watch television hour after hour tend to become passive. The additional athletic events, concerts, the computer, and video games provide an escape from reality and from thinking about life's problems. All this inhibits the building of relationships because spectating limits personal interaction. "Shh, be quiet I'm trying to hear this." How many times have we said this?

The Values of Our Society

A system of values in which material rewards matter more than personal relationships leads to severed relationships. People often move to accept a more highly paid job that will afford them opportunities to have more material rewards. When they move they sever relationships with family, friends, and church. Promotions, status, and pay become determining factors rather than relationships.[1]

To combat the loss of community, some people go to nightclubs; others become overly involved in volunteer organizations. Still others go anywhere they can be around people, such as a daily visit to their bank or a shopping trip to a mall.

People participating in a small group feel wanted when there is a feeling that no one objects to their presence, that they are sincerely welcome, and that they are honestly needed for themselves, not just for their hands or money. The creation of emotional security in a small group, brought about by unconditional love and acceptance, releases people to praise God and grow together. The small group becomes a safe haven where group members can express their deepest struggles without fear of judgment. It is within this context that the church can be all that God planned it to be. "And day by day continuing with one mind in the temple, and breaking bread from house to house, they were taking their meals together with gladness and sincerity of heart, praising God, and having favor with all the people. And the Lord was adding to their number day by day those who were being saved" (Acts 2:46–47, NASB).

A Feeling of Purpose

Does the group work have a real purpose that results in or contributes to basic human welfare and spiritual growth? Does participation in the group result in effects that go beyond the basic group? Participation in a small group must meet these important needs. Essentially a feeling of purpose develops when members understand the biblical reasons for small groups and their participation in them.

The Bible contains many "one another" verses. For instance, God commands us to love one another at least fifty-five times in the New Testament alone. God's intent in these "one another" verses is not simply to give us commands to obey, but to set forth a way of life.

As Christians we cannot grow in Christ if we are isolated from other Christians. Nor can we discover the joyous community of love and Christian victory without the supportive ministry of brothers and sisters in Christ. God expects Christians to band together, caring, loving, and growing into a community in which relationships are not superficial, but penetrating and meaningful—a community in which lifestyles and interpersonal relationships are incorporating "one another" commands.

With all of the "one another" commands in Scripture, there must be some place in the church structure to carry them out. For instance, the Bible commands us to "bear one another's burdens, and thus fulfill the law of Christ" (Gal. 6:2, NASB). But how can we bear one another's burdens if in the church structure there is no opportunity for people to share their burdens?

This is also true of other numerous "one another" commands such as "love one another" (Rom. 13:8), "Be devoted to one another in brotherly love; give preference to one another" (Rom. 12:10, NASB), "have the same care one for another" (1 Cor. 12:25, NASB), and so forth. There is often no setting for people to know one another let alone to care for one another.

Why couldn't these "one another" commands be carried out at periodic church testimony and prayer meetings? Because a larger random group lacks the trust that stems from an interpersonal relationship base that allows one to feel free to share personal burdens, problems, concerns, and victories.

Small groups are a practical expression of love as commanded in 1 John 3:18: "Dear children, let us not love with words or tongue but with actions and in truth." The actions of love are bearing others' burdens, rejoicing with others, sharing insight and lessons learned, edifying one another, helping one another, listening to one another, and sharing goods with one another. Too much of our Bible knowledge is conceptual only. Small groups provide the setting where biblical concepts can become living realities. This is necessary if community is to form. The process of creating community necessitates deep, interpersonal relationships. There are five reasons why small groups are effective:

1. Small Groups Restore Relationships

At the Fall there was a shattering of relationships not only between God and man but between Adam and Eve. When God called to fallen Adam and confronted him, there was an obvious rift in Adam and Eve's relationship. Because of the fall, interpersonal relationships were marred. If man is to function as God has intended, there must be intentional efforts to improve interpersonal relationships. The first and greatest command of a loving God was directed toward the vertical person-God relationship. But the second, "to love your neighbor as yourself," was directed toward the horizontal person-person relationship (Mark 12:30–31).

2. Working Together Is Better Than Working Alone

The combined strength of two is greater than two times the strength of one. Two working together can accomplish more than two working individually. "Two can accomplish more than twice as much as one, for the results can be much better. If one falls, the other pulls him up; but if a man falls when alone, he's in trouble. Also, on a cold night, two under the same blanket gain warmth from each other, but how can one be warm alone?

And one standing alone can be attacked and defeated, but two can stand back-to-back and conquer, three is even better, for a triple-braided cord is not easily broken" (Eccles. 4:9–12, TLB).

3. Jesus Modeled the Use of Small Groups

Jesus modeled the necessity for close personal relationships in his discipling ministry with the twelve apostles. He needed a small support group in Gethsemane as He faced the cross. Just before He went to pray He revealed His inner feelings to Peter, James, and John: "My soul is deeply grieved, to the point of death; remain here and keep watch with Me" (Matt. 26:38, NASB).

4. God Ministers through Groups of People

In Daniel 1:6–21 and 2:17–18 four men banded together (a small group) to maintain their relationship with the Lord and to support one another through prayer. God commands us to relate to other Christians (see Matt. 23:8; John 13:1–17, 34–35). This is because God ministers to people through other people. We need one another to be effective in our world (see 1 Cor. 12:12–27; John 13:34–35; 17:20–23; Matt. 5:13–16). We need one another for personal guidance (Acts 13:1–13; 15:22) and accountability (Luke 19:1–10; 1 Cor. 4:14–21).

5. The "Body" Concept Requires the Small Group

The "body" concept, as set forth in 1 Corinthians 12, indicates that we need each other. Just as there is an interdependency among the physical body members, so is there an interdependency among the members of the body of Christ. To become the people God wants us to become, we need each other. We cannot do it alone.

A Knowledge of What Is Expected

All groups have rules, often called norms. All members agree to abide by these rules while in the group. Members must have a part in determining these rules so they can live and work effectively toward the group goals.

Members must know what the group expects of them in some detail so they can participate in a confident manner. Norms are simply behavior standards to which the participants commit themselves. They are shared expectations of the group. Some of these norms will be mentioned before the group begins; others will be mentioned at the first meeting and be accepted by consensus. All of the participants must commit themselves to these norms if the group is to accomplish its purpose. Standard norms to which most groups agree are as follows.

Regular Participation

Regular participation is necessary if each participant is to build personal relationships that will foster a climate of community. Group members cannot care for, nor be cared for, if they are not spending time together on a regular basis. If a person cannot regularly participate in a group, it is likely that he is not being called of God to join the group and should be asked to wait until he can make a commitment to regular attendance.

Consensus

All major decisions in the group are best made with everyone's feelings considered. Consensus decision making works well since it helps to produce a win-win situation. The vote-and-majority-rule procedure thrusts the group into a win-lose situation. Instead of being cared for, the loser is often hurt. Helpful questions members of the group could ask each other are "What would help you?" and "How would you feel if . . .?" Then present alternatives or adjustments that are acceptable to the group.

Honesty

Honesty means freedom to communicate real feelings and beliefs on any issue. There are three levels of communication between persons.

Level 1: Mouth-to-Mouth Communication. This basic level is the most frequently used. It is expressed in phrases such as "How are you?", "How's it going?", and "Good to see you." These phrases keep communication open but are very superficial. When these phrases are used, even though some are questions, an honest response is not expected. The person asking does not really want you to tell him about all the problems you have.

Level 2: Head-to-Head Communication. This is the communication of ideas from one person to another. Such communication is important for interpersonal relationships but still is not the level of communication that enables mutual caring.

Level 3: Heart-to-Heart Communication. Here superficiality is absent, and one can honestly and openly share deep feelings. This kind of honest sharing is the mark of New Testament *koinonia* or "fellowship." "But if we walk in the light [purity and honesty before God and man], as he is in the light, we have fellowship with one another, and the blood of Jesus, his Son, purifies us from all sin" (1 John 1:7). This is an intimate kind of sharing that is done only with a small number of people with whom a mutual level of trust and a sense of community have been developed.

Confidentiality

Absolute confidentiality is an indispensable norm. If people are sharing their feelings, shortcomings, failures, sins, and struggles, they must be able to trust the group members to keep their confidence. Without this trust the relationships will not grow strong and the small group will not be successful.

Acceptance

Accepting people where they are is necessary in a small group. Immaturity, different viewpoints, failures, weaknesses, and shortcomings in other people tend to make us want to change or reject them. As we grow in Christ, we often become critical of those who have not yet "attained" our level. Setting the atmosphere to accept one another is essential. This is the way God accepts us as we are.

Active Listening

When someone is sharing a problem, group members must resist the temptation to become advice givers. Instead they must listen actively. Active listening involves asking questions to draw out the individual and help him to express his problem and to encourage him to continue seeking the solution to the problem. Active listening involves body language that indicates you care and are sincerely interested in a person's problem. Poor body language would consist of yawning, looking at your watch, looking away, and anything else that expresses lack of interest and genuine caring.

Prayer

Each person in the group should commit to pray regularly for every other group member. This is important because God is our only help to give victory over sin, to supply every need, and to solve every problem.

Punctuality

Each group member must arrive on time, and the group must begin on time and end on time. Each session should last no more than two hours, including refreshments. Commitment to regular participation is easier when there is assurance that the schedule will be adhered to.

Positive Attitude

Small groups are to be affirming and encouraging. Since the goal is to build each other up, members should work together to create a positive atmosphere and to lift up the church, their leaders, their policies, and one another.

A Part in Planning the Group's Goals

People need to have a part in the structuring of the overall group's plans and goals. This need is satisfied when their ideas have a fair hearing. Questions group members should ask are: "Is progress being made toward the overall group goals?" or "Are the meetings simply going nowhere?" Goals and plans must be within reach. If members sense that the plans are beyond a reasonable ability to be reached, they will lose heart in the group.

A Challenging Atmosphere

Time is becoming an increasingly precious commodity. People are becoming increasingly conscious of how they use their time. They will stay involved in groups that use their gifts and challenge their thinking. They must sense that they are challenged within the range of their abilities and interests and that their work in the group will lead them to accomplish the group's goals.

An Understanding of What Is Going On

Small group members need to be kept informed. What people are not informed about they often oppose. Keeping members informed is one way to give them status as individuals. Leaders usually think they have communicated, but those who listen sometimes find they do not understand what is being asked or stated.

At the height of the vacation season one year, a trained investigator mingled with the crowds at Grand Central Station in New York City. He asked ten people, "What is your destination?" He got these replies:

1. Protestant.

2. Mind your own business.

3. I'm a shoe salesman.

4. Home, if I can find my wife.

5. I'm learning to be a mail clerk.

6. Checkers.

7. Shut your mouth!

8. I don't know you.

9. Hoboken.

10. I believe in faith, hope, and charity to all.[2]

Obviously, we must never assume we have communicated to the members of our group. Get feedback. Make certain you're understood.

Do We Have the Sense of a Goose?

In the fall when you see geese flying south for the winter, they will most likely be in a "V" formation. Science discovered sometime ago that they fly that way for a purpose. As each bird flaps its wings, it creates an uplift for the bird immediately behind. By using this flying formation, the entire flock adds about 71 percent greater flying range than if each bird flew on its own.

When a goose falls out of formation, it suddenly feels the drag of trying to go it alone and quickly returns to the formation to take advantage of the lifting power of the flock. As the lead goose gets tired, he rotates back in the formation and another goose flies the point. The geese honk from behind to encourage those up front to keep up their speed.

If a goose becomes sick or wounded and falls out of formation, two geese fall out and follow him down to provide assistance and protection. They stay with the fallen goose until he is restored to health, and then together they launch out with another formation to catch up with the group.

If we have the sense of a goose, we will learn three things from this story about creating community:

1. We need a common sense of direction, so we can get where we are going faster by traveling on the thrust of one another.

2. We must stay together, taking turns doing difficult jobs and encouraging those who are leading the way.

3. We need to stand by each other, helping and protecting one another until we all can move forward together.[3]

Negative and Positive Conditions of Community

Negative Conditions	Positive Conditions
1. aggressive or hostile atmosphere	1. friendly, accepting atmosphere
2. prestige-seeking	2. collaboration-seeking
3. hostility to change	3. supportive of change
4. individualistic, unshared goals	4. commonly shared goals
5. using the group for ego satisfaction	5. using the group for growth
6. goals developed by one	6. goals developed by all
7. focused only on activity	7. focused on results
8. group sets up a standard ritual that never changes	8. group changes its operation as needs arise
9. only a polite friendliness allowed	9. group expresses various moods (tension, concern, etc.)
10. time seen as an obstacle ("there's not enough time")	10. time seen as a tool ("how can we make the most of our time?")
11. satisfied with appearance of progress	11. only satisfied with progress toward group goals
12. group discourages personal growth	12. group allows members to grow
13. members do not identify with the group—it is just another group	13. members personally identify with the group—its continuance is important to them
14. results viewed as the responsibility of the leader of the group	14. results viewed as the responsibility of all members of the group
15. superficial, irrelevant talk	15. purposeful, relevant talk
16. specialized jargon	16. common, understandable language
17. information kept hidden	17. information freely distributed
18. feelings not expressed	18. feelings expressed

CHAPTER FOUR

A Healthy Start

The artist visualizes the picture before it goes on the canvas. The pilot sees the landing in all its dimensions before the wheels touch the ground. The professional golfer pictures the swing and the shot before striking the ball.

The lesson is clear. We must visualize in our hearts and minds exactly what our new small group ministry will look like when it is completed.

What Is a Small Group?

A small group is a face-to-face gathering of three to twelve people on a regular time schedule during which a sense of accountability to each other and Jesus Christ is present. Notice four elements in this definition.

1. Face-to-face: people interface with each other directly and personally.

2. Three to twelve people: the group is small enough for face-to-face relationships to take place.

3. Regular time schedule: the group meets at least twice a month.

4. Sense of accountability: the group members have a feeling of concern and responsibility for each other.

A Means to an End

To build a strong small group ministry that will lead groups in fulfilling this characterization, you must build from the bottom up rather than trying to dictate from the top down. You must resist the pressure to go public with your small group ministry before you get the necessary infrastructure in place to support the ministry.

Remember that small groups are not your ultimate goal. Small groups are only a means to get to your goal. Do not lose your sense of direction. The Christian life is not a solo journey. In order for Joshua to be victorious he needed the support of Moses, Aaron, and Hur. In order for us to be victorious in our Christian lives we need the support of brothers and sisters in Jesus Christ who lift their hands "up to the throne of the Lord" on our behalf.

> The Amalekites came and attacked the Israelites at Rephidim. Moses said to Joshua, "Choose some of our men and go out to fight the Amalekites. Tomorrow I will stand on top of the hill with the staff of God in my hands."
>
> So Joshua fought the Amalekites as Moses had ordered, and Moses, Aaron and Hur went to the top of the hill. As long as Moses held up his hands, the Israelites were winning, but whenever he lowered his hands, the Amalekites were winning. When Moses' hands grew tired, they took a stone and put it under him and he sat on it. Aaron and Hur held his hands up—one on one side, one on the other—so that his hands remained steady till sunset. So Joshua overcame the Amalekite army with the sword. . . .
>
> Moses built an altar and called it The LORD is my Banner. He said, "For hands were lifted up to the throne of the LORD." (Exod. 17:8–13, 15–16)

We need one another!

Look before You Leap

As previously noted, ministry and personal growth are most effectively accomplished through a company of believers who are committed to Christ, to one another, and to ministry in the world.

Begin small groups that promote the basic values of your church. If the small group model you employ excludes worship or fellowship, that model will violate the essential values of your church right from the start. Whatever type or style of small groups you choose to use, they must be faithful to your core values.

Recognize that some small group training models won't fit certain kinds of churches and cultural situations. There are many ways to do a small group ministry. You may have read about a church that built a significant ministry around small groups. Though it worked for the originator, it won't necessarily work for you without some modifications. For example, people working in a blue-collar setting may find they need more structure to their small groups. Those ministering in a white-collar situation often find their groups need more freedom.

Some pastors assume that every person who worships at their Sunday church services should be in a small group. Experience has shown this to be naive. Younger people tend to desire a high "quantity" of relationships with just a few close friends. As people age they often prefer to develop deeper relationships with fewer people. Those nearing retirement often find it difficult to involve themselves in small groups with a high turnover. It's too hard for them to undergo so much social change.

In most cases you should launch small groups over a period of time. To suddenly announce, "Next week, we're going to divide everyone into small groups" can be disruptive and hurtful. It is wise for a leader to give the process at least a year, if not longer, in older, established churches. Give people lots of time to buy into or out of the ministry. Share literature with leaders so they can become acquainted with small group ministry. Take members to workshops or seminars on small groups to help them understand what groups are all about. Visit some nearby churches that are already successfully using small groups as an important part of their church ministry.

Nine Types of Small Groups

Plan on using a variety of small groups. Most churches have experienced only one type of group: the Bible study. While this is a key type of group, it is only one of at least nine types.

1. Bible Study Groups

Bible studies usually focus on learning and applying what the Bible says. The focus is often on a particular book of the Bible or a specific topic. Typically, each person is assigned homework during the week and is expected to complete their assignments before their small group needs.

2. Prayer Groups

While the group may spend some time studying what the Bible or a writer says *about* prayer, the objective of the prayer group is to spend time *in* prayer. Members expect God to act on their behalf and are not surprised to find that their prayers are answered.

3. Fellowship Groups

These groups stress social interaction and provide a place for people to get acquainted. Many times they are organized around age, personal interest, or life stages.

4. Task Groups

Task groups exist to serve others. Most people bond better if they share a common goal or activity. Thus, when a group serves others (e.g., ministering to the poor, prisoners, sick, etc.), they both perform a task and develop a high degree of love and acceptance for one another.

5. Training Groups

These groups are usually short term, only lasting until a specific skill has been taught. A group might meet for one or two months to work on character formation. Perhaps a group of new believers meets for six weeks to discuss the beginning of their Christian faith. These groups can be much fun and can help initiate people into other small groups where deeper participation and sharing take place.

6. Accountability Groups

People attending an accountability group are very serious about applying the Word of God to their personal lives. They give other group members permission to hold them accountable for their Christian walk. This has become increasingly popular in men's groups today with the Promise Keepers movement gaining momentum.

7. Integration Groups

These groups assist newcomers to get involved in the life of the church. Since solid relationships are the key to keeping people in any church, such groups are vital to a growing, healthy church. Newcomers come to a church for many different reasons, but they usually stay because they make a close friend in the church.[1]

8. Covenant Groups

The main purpose of a covenant group is to be obedient to Christ. Most covenant groups write a "covenant" that specifically details their commitment to the Lord and each other. All members of the group sign the covenant and seriously seek to fulfill it.

9. House Church Groups

These groups function as a church by experiencing all the normal church functions including baptism, the Lord's Supper, corporate worship, and financial giving. These groups often grow to include fifty people and see themselves as more than a small group. In members' minds, they are the church.

Be Prepared for These Eight Problems before You Start

Be realistic about the spiritual climate of your church. Spiritual leaders are not immune to problems. It should come as no surprise to realize that we are not perfect. Below are some internal and external problems common to spiritual leadership. If these problems exist in your church, it is highly likely they will undermine any effort to begin a small group ministry. Thus, it is wise to work on overcoming these eight problems before beginning your small group ministry.[2]

Problem 1: Church Leaders with Poor Self-Image

Church leaders are often plagued with insecurities and doubts about their leadership. They are unable to trust others because they fear disloyalty. In most cases, leaders who have a deep-seated sense of inadequacy seek to control all aspects of small group ministry, and, in so doing, undermine the freedom and flexibility to allow the small group ministry to flourish. Such insecure leaders cite fears such as the possibility of small groups getting into doctrinal error or splitting off from the mother church as reasons for their high control. Indeed there have been instances where small groups have been less than ideal, but research will point out the fact that such instances are overexaggerated. The bottom line in most situations is that the leaders are simply insecure in their own self-image.

It is wise for all leaders to remember that God chooses to use the weak, base, and foolish things to bring glory to Himself (1 Cor. 1:26–28). Paul boasted in his weakness because it caused him to rely on Christ's power and strength and not his own (2 Cor. 12:9–10). Whatever a spiritual leader needs, Christ is able to supply. The spiritual leader must avoid the common mistake of either demanding more of himself than the Lord is asking of him or allowing himself to become enslaved to other people's expectations of him rather than the Lord's.

Problem 2: Fear of Failure

Some leaders hesitate to begin or support small groups in their church because they are afraid that such a ministry will fail. It could be that a small group ministry was attempted previously and was unsuccessful. This failure may have inoculated them: they experienced just enough of the ministry to keep them from trying again.

Paul spoke to such leaders when he told Timothy, "For God has not given us a spirit of timidity, but of power and love and discipline" (2 Tim. 1:7, NASB). If after you have made a sound investigation into the need for small groups, it seems like the right thing to do, then you must do it. Expect to make mistakes. If you never attempt anything for God, you will never make a mistake. Step out and trust God's guidance as you attempt great things for Him. When you do make mistakes, be quick to learn from them and avoid repeating them.

Problem 3: Discouragement and Disappointment

A discouraged church finds it hard to begin any new ministry. If your church recently experienced a heavy disappointment, don't try to begin your new small group ministry until after a period of healing.

A church where Gary served as pastor was located on a small parcel of about 1.5 acres, which cramped growth by severely limiting off-street parking. Over a period of several months, the church board worked to acquire a larger property of about five acres. The move to the new location would have given the church room to expand and continue its growth. Church members were enthusiastic about buying the new property, and 98 percent voted in favor of relocating—a small miracle in itself! However, the deal fell through, and the resultant discouragement that set in led to several years of frustration.

Rare is the church and leader that do not get discouraged and disappointed at times. Things do not always turn out the way we expect. Church leaders must keep their eyes on Christ instead of themselves, others, or circumstances. Those who are able to assist a church to trust God with great faith will be on their way to effectively handling such discouragement and disappointment.

Problem 4: Spiritual Dryness

Walk into any church you are not accustomed to attending and you will immediately notice the prevailing atmosphere. In some churches you can feel the enthusiasm, excitement, and joy. In others you feel dullness, anger, or apathy.

Lack of power in a church is usually caused by an absence of vital prayer, commitment to studying and living God's Word, holy living, or a sense of purpose and vision. Church leaders must focus on reviving the church's spiritual life before instituting a small group ministry. Small groups can be an aid in renewing a church's spiritual energy due to the personal care, study of God's Word, and prayer that they encourage. However, a spiritually dry church will often find it must begin the effort for small groups slowly.

Problem 5: Poor Time Management

Small groups add to the complexity of a church by making it necessary to manage more people, space, and time. A church that struggles with time management should not begin a small group ministry until it gets its current time management under control.

Beginning a small group ministry often requires major shifts in commitments and priorities. An all-church calendar and schedule is absolutely necessary for a smooth-running small group ministry. Having a schedule and going over it regularly with other leaders will help eliminate some time management problems. Regularly defining ministry and life priorities and keeping faithful to them is important to the scheduling process.

Problem 6: Relational Conflicts

When you work with lumber, you will inevitably get some splinters in your hands. When you work with people, you will have some conflicts. Most of these conflicts, like splinters, are fairly minor. But sometimes the conflict becomes so painful that all work stops. It's like hitting your thumb with a hammer. Immediately all other bodily functions seem to cease as you hold your thumb. It's literally impossible to keep working until the pain goes away. Some relational conflicts are like hitting our thumbs. We must stop whatever ministry function is going on until we deal with the problem.

Personality clashes, jealousy over roles or abilities, competitiveness, and being threatened by others' gifts or ministries are a few of the relational problems that can bring effective ministry to a halt. We need to see others as better than ourselves and desire to see them succeed in what they are doing. Before a successful small group ministry can be developed, leaders begin praying for each other. They repent of unloving attitudes and behaviors. They rejoice in what God is doing in and through each person in their church. They eliminate the ministry-stopping relational conflicts so that God's ministry can move forward.

Problem 7: Overload and Burnout

In our "Finding Them, Keeping Them Seminar," we ask participants to make a list of all the ministries that take place weekly at their church. Most people are surprised at the large number of things going on at their church. After reading over their list, they know why they are so tired.

A few years ago, Dr. Win Arn conducted a survey to discover how much time people have for structured ministry in addition to attending Sunday morning services. He discovered that we have an average of only three hours to give to ministry each week. See figure below.

Figure 5

Weekly time for structured ministry
outside of Sunday morning

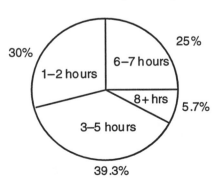

Obviously, people in our busy society don't have much time to devote to attending meetings or programs. Churches that expect people to attend practically every time the doors of the church are open will find people experiencing burnout. If your members and worshipers are reluctant to participate because their schedules at work and at home are already over-loaded, you will find it hard to get a small group ministry started.

Problems do result from overextending ourselves and taking on more than we can adequately handle. At the personal level, this can be solved by learning to delegate responsibilities to others. At the church level it may be necessary to cut back on activities the Lord has not called us to or which have lost their effectiveness. Before beginning a small group ministry, church leaders should assess their church programs, functions, and ministries against the overall purpose of the church. If beginning a small group ministry is viewed as crucial to fulfilling your purpose, you may have to eliminate some other church functions in order to make time for small groups.

Problem 8: Conflict with Authority

Small group ministries have experienced a very high success rate in Asian churches. One of the reasons is due to the high respect given to leaders within the Asian culture. The Asian culture tends to emphasize corporate identity rather than individual identity. Thus, what is best for the family or church receives a higher priority than what is best for the individual. It is important to give honor to those in leadership. Thus, what the leader determines is best for the church (or group) is received as from the Lord.

Our Western culture stresses the individual more than the group. What is best for the individual receives a higher priority than what is best for the group. And leaders are not as honored, but questioned and challenged. This makes small group ministry slightly harder to develop in a Western culture.

In most churches this challenge to leadership is handled well and poses no major difficulty in beginning a small group ministry. However, problems arise when people act independently of God-anointed authority. Churches that have a recent history of conflict with leadership will no doubt find it best to wait before beginning small groups. Rebellious attitudes and actions should be repented of, and spiritual leaders should be given respect. Without such mutual submission, small groups will not grow as they should.

CHAPTER FIVE

Evaluate the Climate for Change

A number of years back the *London Times* ran a front-page story about an Englishman named Arthur Arch. He had just celebrated his ninety-fifth birthday, which was an accomplishment in and of itself. However, the truly newsworthy thing about Mr. Arch was that for the past forty-two years, he had been precisely and consistently twenty minutes late for every meeting and appointment. According to his own time, he was always prompt. But according to everyone else's time, he was always late!

In 1922 in England all the clocks had been changed by twenty minutes. We have no idea why, but we do know that Mr. Arch never accepted the change. In fact, he said: "Nobody is going to take twenty minutes off my life. So, I'll keep my watch at the old standard time. And someday I plan to die twenty minutes late just to prove that I was right!"

Mr. Arch had an American counterpart who was a very stubborn man, a Kansas farmer and an independent thinker if there ever was one. His name has been lost, but in the early 1940s this Kansas farmer alleged that the worst thing that ever happened in the United States of America was the election of Franklin Delano Roosevelt as president. He believed that the worst thing Roosevelt ever did was to approve the law establishing daylight savings time.

After the law was passed, the farmer never changed his clocks. He was always one half hour off the time observed by everyone else during daylight savings time. Like Arthur Arch, he lived and died by the old time. His defense, he felt, was theological. He once said, "I will not exchange God's time for Roosevelt's time!"[1]

The parallels between a story like this and the church of the nineties are numerous. Any church that refuses to keep up with the time is always going to be a little behind in its efforts to reach its community. People who hinder change will often be left behind because of their own stubbornness and traditionalism. Are you genuinely committed to the Great Commission? Is your church willing to do whatever it takes to fulfill God's greatest decree for the church in your generation? Paul was. He said, "I have become all things to all men so that by all possible means I might save some" (1 Cor. 9:22).

Evaluating Your Readiness

A church must be fully prepared and motivated to be able to establish a small group ministry that will be effective and efficient. To this end we have created a test to help you determine both the "will" and the "skill" of your church to start a small group ministry. To gain the most insight from this tool, be honest about the climate in your church. When you answer, think of how your church would be most likely to answer as an entire corporation. Answer True or False to each statement below.

Evaluating Your Will

TRUE/FALSE

1. Our church desires to see newcomers stay and get involved. _____

2. When new programs are instituted, small groups are always a part of the planning. _____

3. The people in our church recognize that pastoral care is not efficient on a lay level. _____

4. We have never had a small group ministry begin and fail due to a lack of interest. _____

5. Small groups are an active part of the senior pastor's vision. _____

6. We have determined that our Sunday school program is not meeting the basic needs of support and belonging in our people's lives. _____

7. Small groups are *not* seen as a threat to presently established ministries. _____

8. Small groups are listed as a line item in our church budget. _____

9. Our church has trouble enlisting volunteers and workers for church ministry. _____

10. We have identified a large number of members who seek counseling from outside sources or agencies. _____

11. Many people in the church have verbalized their desire for a small group ministry. _____

12. We have noticed an increase in the number of people who once attended our church but are now going elsewhere. _____

13. The pastor(s) and leaders are willing to be involved in starting and modeling small groups. _____

14. The members of the congregation have more personal issues in their lives than can be addressed on a Sunday morning. _____

15. Most people are in basic agreement with the current direction of our church. _____

Total Checked True _____

Evaluating Your Skill

TRUE/FALSE

1. Fifty percent of our members have received training on how to care for one another. _____

2. Our church has identified one strong leader or couple for every ten people. _____

3. Our church has several unofficial small group meetings throughout the week. _____

4. We have an assimilation strategy in place that includes small groups. _____

5. Church leadership is committed to a diverse ministry to the meet needs of all our people. _____

6. Fifty percent of the current leadership has been trained or discipled in a small group setting. _____

7. Our church has a staff person who has been trained in small group dynamics. _____

8. We offer regularly scheduled small group training events. _____

9. Our people trust the leadership and staff along with the vision they have communicated. _____

10. A significant number of members have volunteered to lead a group when we start small groups. _____

11. Ten percent or more of the people of our church have been involved in small groups and small group leadership in the past. _____

12. Five to ten percent of the church members have attended some kind of small group training event. _____

13. We presently have trained laypeople doing one-on-one discipleship. _____

14. Our church has many people who participate in secular support and recovery groups. _____

15. The leadership team has several professionals who are adept at leading groups of people and are willing to share their expertise. _____

Total Checked True _____

Now, to see what kind of church you are working with, plot your answers on figure 6. Circle the number of TRUE answers to the "will" portion of the test on the vertical line. Then circle the number of TRUE answers from the "skill" portion of the test on the horizontal line. Draw two straight lines, perpendicular from each circled number, until they connect. For example, a church may have had eight answers marked TRUE under "will" and five answers marked TRUE under "skill." The sample below shows how its grid would look when completed. The church would be in section 2, which represents the "Dedicated Church."

Sample

Figure 6

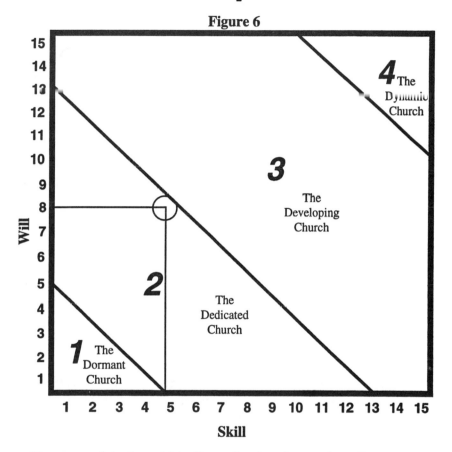

Now, complete the grid in figure 7 using the numbers from your own answers to the questionnaire. What section does your church fall into?

The point where the two lines connect will be in one of the four sections above. The first section (1) represents the "Dormant Church." This has nothing to do with the state of the people attending worship services or prayer meeting. This church simply lacks both the will and the skill to launch a fully developed small group program, and therefore it will need

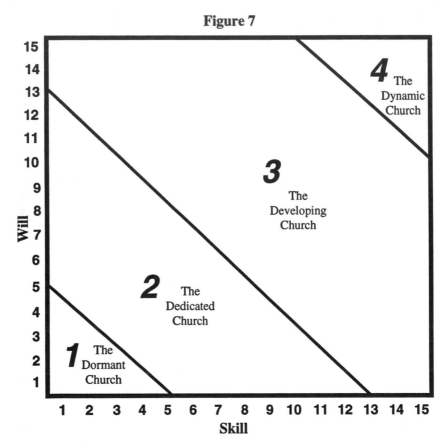

Figure 7

to take specific steps to prepare itself for this new ministry if success is to be expected. Chapter 6 is designed to enable the church to take such steps.

The second section (2) represents the "Dedicated Church." This church has identified some skills for small group ministries and a little will to create such a program. However, if your church falls into this area, it probably is apparent that the whole church has not yet seen the benefits of the program or there is skepticism about the outcome. The church is dedicated to the process of bringing new people to Christ and assimilating them into the body. It also needs to evaluate what steps are necessary to make small groups successful in that particular congregation. Chapter 7 will empower you to make the needed changes in preparing for small groups.

The third section (3) represents the "Developing Church." This is the church that both is open to new ideas and has the foundational skills and leadership to innovate a new small group ministry. Chapter 8 has been designed to help you determine the best timing and process for small groups while taking advantage of the apparent readiness of the church.

Lastly, the fourth section (4) represents the "Dynamic Church." If your church is in this category, chapter 9 will help you see the specific keys to starting and maintaining the energy that already has been established in the church with small groups.

Our church's potential falls into
the category of a _____church.

Churches that find themselves in the lower two sections (1 and 2) usually find the Slow Track Model (described in chap. 10) as the best way to begin a small group ministry. Those churches that are in the upper two sections (3 and 4) can use effectively the Fast Track Model (described in chap. 11).

Discovering Your Achilles' Heel

The concept of an Achilles' heel comes from the Greek myth of the great warrior Achilles. According to the legend, when Achilles' mother dipped him in a river to make him invulnerable, the water washed every part except the heel by which she had held him. Thus the one weak spot, his heel, was both the proof of his humanity and his potential downfall. Rather than accepting his vulnerability and learning from it, Achilles defiantly tried to prove he was invincible. He repeatedly exposed himself to attack, winning several battles before his bitter rival Paris shot a fatal arrow at his heel.

Poor Achilles was doomed to have an unchangeable fatal flaw. For unbelievers, this is a very appropriate illustration of how their weaknesses cannot permanently be changed by their own strength. But for believers it is an entirely different story. We may start out with an Achilles' heel, but with God's help we can overcome any weakness, as Paul points out in Philippians 4:13.

So for our purposes here, an Achilles' heel is a reference to the part of a person, or in this context, the church, that is both our greatest handicap and our greatest challenge. If we accept and learn, it will become a source of strength and guidance with the Lord's help. If we fail to learn from our weaknesses, as many churches have, we will struggle, and our weakness will continue to reappear at times when we least expect it, such as the starting of new ministries.

Over the past twenty-five years of ministry, we have seen the Achilles' heel of most churches fall into one or more of the categories of Four Paralyzing Fears: (1) Fear of Change, (2) Fear of Failure, (3) Fear of the Truth, and (4) Fear of Control. Let's briefly evaluate each of these potential problems.

Four Paralyzing Fears

1. Fear of Change

All of us reach a point in our lives when we fear change. Change is welcomed as a child because change is merely a demonstration of growth. We make a little mark on the wall each year to measure our change in height. We graduate from one stage of education to the next, which is another sign of growth. As we reach adulthood, especially our middle years, change is no longer welcomed. Height no longer is the concern, but width. No longer in school, we have no advancements to anticipate. We just want life to remain in the status quo, secure and constant. It's at this point we must remember that change is necessary for growth and, despite our fears, change is good. As change is introduced into the church, we must be reeducated to the cyclical nature and progression of change as seen in the figure below.

Figure 8

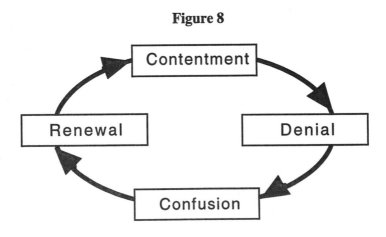

Because we are human we are content with life as it is. We want life to stay comfortable and calm. When change is introduced it is often hard to accept, and denial results. We don't like it. We're afraid of it so we fight it. The result? Confusion. "Why are we starting these groups anyway? Things have been going along just fine." "What is the leadership trying to do, destroy the church? Don't they understand that cliques are going to form and we won't get to know everyone?" To move past these stages of denial and confusion takes patience and communication. The result will be a sense of renewal that eventually will cycle back to the contentment we all desire. We must not allow a fear of change to become an Achilles' heel, revealing a weakness inherent in many churches. Methods will change. Programs must change. But we can all praise God that He is unchanging and His message needs to be treated the same.

2. Fear of Failure

Our families went on vacation together in 1990 to Colorado, where we decided to take a river rafting expedition, a half day of braving the wilds of white water. We did not allow any fear of potential problems to get in our way. We approached the adventure with great expectations and excitement. Although the rapids we had chosen were very mild, we still experienced the thrill of the raft bucking and pitching. At one point in particular, both of us remember that all paddling ceased, and we concentrated on just keeping the raft from turning sideways and toppling over as we hit one turn known as "the wall." It was at this point that the river became a real equalizer. We were all in this raft together, and we all had to start rowing and sharing the responsibility, or we could be in trouble. So, we rowed together, we steered together, and we had a lot of fun—together.

This is the power of vision. A vision unites people. A vision provides people with something to aim at and move toward. *It gives them hope.* Sadly, few churches have any real sense of direction. Therefore they find that when small groups are introduced, no one can articulate why they could be beneficial to the church and why the church should rally behind this ministry and how. Many will fear that small groups may fail as they have in the past. Such fear can paralyze the church from ever experiencing the great benefit of the unified vision small groups can provide.

3. Fear of the Truth

Ostriches are very interesting animals. When faced with a test or a pending problem, their plan of attack is to hide their heads in the sand for protection. Their approach is like many churches. "If we ignore it, maybe it will go away." We are sorry to say that problems do not always go away by themselves, and ignoring them will not help. *We have to face the truth if we are to survive and prosper.* To ignore the changes in people's lives, the changes in culture, the new thinking of the boomers and busters with the incredible schedules of life today, is to hide your head in the sand and hope for yesterday to return. It is to be paralyzed by the fear of looking at what is true and then dealing with what you see. The healthy church is willing to examine what is true and act accordingly, even if this means embracing the truth and doing things differently than they have been done in the past.

In our book, *The Issachar Factor,* we wrote, "Let's face it: Most church models of ministry were developed in an entirely different age. The models of ministry developed in the agricultural and industrial ages are colliding head-on with the information age. . . . Our nation has changed; people have changed; and we must develop new models of ministry relevant for today's society if we are to fulfill Christ's commission to 'make disciples.'"[2]

To fail to look at our times and desire to evaluate the church's readiness to meet these challenges is to put our heads in the sand.

4. Fear of Control

Several control factors can become Achilles' heels and produce paralyzing fear. There is the fear of losing control of the Christian education of the church. "Will we be destroying the Sunday school program by starting small groups?" "Will any of these small groups fall into doctrinal error because the leaders are not seminary trained?" Granting that doctrine must continue to be a high priority, there is no fear of losing control if small groups are managed correctly.

We must not forget the fear of losing control of the church's follower-ship. By *follower-ship,* we mean the desire of the church in general to follow the leading of the staff and governing board. When small groups are initiated, you begin the process of delegating responsibility and authority to people, other than key leadership, to govern a small body of believers. Some churches prevent this from happening by mandating that all small groups must be led by an elder or deacon or staff person. This controlling factor will prove to limit leadership development.

There is also the loss of control for the pastoral care of the people. This can be viewed as a welcome loss, when the people begin to care for one another in a preventative way rather than the pastor having the sole responsibility of caring for the flock in a more reactive sense. But when the staff is no longer called upon in times of crisis, this can be very threatening for the church and its leadership. Thus, fear can paralyze in many different ways, but no matter how it does, it ends up hurting the church and keeping it from all God has for it to do and become.

An Opportunity for Growth

Far from being an obstacle, our Achilles' heel can serve as an opportunity for improving our church's ministry. The good news is that by discovering and coming to grips with our weaknesses, biases, and fears, we can make our church's self-defeating behavior less automatic, less resistant to change, and more quickly resolvable. For instance, an Achilles' heel may become an early warning sign that some area of ministry needs more attention.

Never forget that growth is not linear in the church; it resembles more of a stairway.

Figure 9

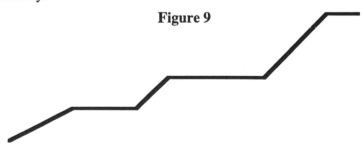

The church tends to grow for a period of time and then plateaus in preparation for the next stage of leadership development. Instead of getting frustrated when a time of plateauing arrives due to your Achilles' heel, use this time to reinforce support and learn to see this segment of church life as a period of preparation for the future. Please understand that whatever receives your attention can grow stronger. If the church weaknesses are seen as unmanageable flaws, an aura of dismay and lack of hope will develop. If seen as an opportunity to grow and mature, the church's self-image can be raised, and there will be increased satisfaction as plateaus are overcome.

Don't Get Skunked

The story is told of a young family on vacation. This family loved camping and enjoyed the times of getting together, setting up the campsite, and building campfires. This family had a dog that they always brought along, not wanting to place it in a kennel.

One night, just as the family was dozing off, the dog went crazy. She barked and snapped at the chain that anchored her to the campsite, just trying to go after something she sensed in the dark. After a few minutes of discussing who would go out and brave the cold to check on the dog, the dad peeked through the tent doorway to detect the unmistakable odor of a skunk. Needless to say, he never left the tent, and the dog quieted down after some consoling.

The next evening at dusk, the family was walking back slowly from their evening shower routine, and just ahead they saw a lantern bobbing up and down as someone was running along holding it. As they neared the light, they were able to detect another couple in pursuit of the then familiar black-and-white-striped garbage thieves of the campground.

Dad's first thought was that these people were even dumber than his dog. Then he wondered if they were from the city and had no idea what was in store for them. Finally, he turned to the rest of his family and asked, "Now, just what are they going to do if they catch it?"

The analogy is pretty obvious. People in churches and leadership of churches spend hours, days, and years chasing things and programs they don't fully understand or support. But they will never be happy until they do catch them! So much of what we see churches pursuing has little Kingdom impact and lasting results. In the end, many churches just feel like they've been skunked. You can do a lot of things, but you can be most successful by doing the right things. The right things necessary to integrate small groups into the life of your church depend on the category of church you have just discovered. Turn now to the chapter that bears the name of the category your church falls into and discover what the right things are for your church.

CHAPTER SIX

The Dormant Church

In American church life today, we find many churches just "faking it." The majority of growth in churches throughout the country today is *transfer growth,* people leaving one church and going to another. American demographics reveal that giving is down, serving in ministries is down, and frustration is up. So, some kind of turning point will be absolutely vital if a church is to turn the corner from being a dormant church to becoming a developing church. This was the kind of turning point encountered by Roy Robertson more than fifty years ago:

My ship, the *U.S.S. Vega,* docked at Pearl Harbor on the evening of December 6, 1941. A couple of the fellows and I left the ship that night and attended a Bible study. About fifteen sailors sat in a circle on the floor. The leader asked us to each recite our favorite Scripture verse. In turn each sailor shared a verse and briefly commented on it. I sat there in terror. I couldn't recall a single verse. I grew up in a Christian home, went to church three times a week, but I sat there terrified. I couldn't recall a single verse. Finally, I remembered one verse—John 3:16. I silently rehearsed it in my mind.

The spotlight of attention grew closer as each sailor took his turn. It was up to the fellow next to me. He recited John 3:16. He took my verse! As he commented on it I sat there in stunned humiliation. In a few moments everyone would know that I could not recall from memory even a single verse. Later that night I went to bed thinking, "Robertson, you're a fake."

At 7:55 the next morning I was awakened by the ship alarm ordering us to battle stations. Three hundred sixty planes of the Japanese Imperial Fleet were attacking our ship and the other military installations. My crew and I raced to our machine gun emplacement, but all we had was practice ammunition. So for the first fifteen minutes of the two-hour battle, we only fired blanks hoping to scare the Japanese airplanes. As I stood there firing fake ammunition I thought, "Robertson, this is how your whole life has been—firing blanks for Christ." I made up my mind as Japanese bullets slammed into our ship, "If I escape with my life, I will get serious about following Jesus."[1]

Roy Robertson went on to help Dawson Trotman found the Navigators. Robertson led the follow-up ministry for the 1990 Billy Graham Crusade in Hong Kong. That crusade found more people hearing the gospel at one time than any other meeting in history. Roy Robertson had to awaken to the reality that he had been faking it in his spiritual life far too long and it was time to change. If your church falls into the Dormant category, you must do the same.

The Key to Health: Renewal of the Spiritual Life

A church that falls into the category of a Dormant Church faces what appears to be an uphill battle. As we have pointed out, it lacks both the will and the skill to launch a fully developed small group program and will need to take specific steps to be successful in this new ministry. There will likely be some old wounds that will need to be dealt with. Small groups will aid in the healing process for such a church. Before implementing the groups, there are nine action steps this church will need to accomplish if it is serious about creating community through a small group ministry.

Action Step 1: Recognize the Reasons for Dormancy

In the history of any church, the student of church growth will identify patterns of growth and decline. There are two items that must come high on the agenda of any church longing to make a difference in the world. First you will need to recognize your need by looking at your current situation and the past history of the church. Then take the step of repentance to correct these weaknesses and strongholds of the Enemy that are keeping you from reaching God's highest purposes for your church.

These steps are not optional. They can and most likely will be painful, yet they will result in healing. Realize that if you were to add only extra programming, without addressing the underlying causes for your present condition, the results would be minimal at best. It would be like putting a bandage over a sliver instead of removing the sliver first. So we suggest you bite the bullet and implement the following actions.

As you approach this task, it is important to go to the Lord and ask Him to give you insight into the dynamics in your church's history that will help you recognize what needs to be done to correct the problems. You should commit yourselves as leaders to be absolutely honest and transparent before the Lord in taking ownership as a congregation for what the Lord shows. You may want to contact "old-timers" and former pastors who may have retired or moved but may be able to give information and insights. Talking with "old timers" (who are not part of the problems) and former pastors or parishioners may prove to be a good source for identifying problems or clarifying existing ones. Figure 10 is an example of how to list these significant events in the life of your church.

Figure 10

Noteworthy Events in the Church's History
1977 - Church is founded after a split
1978 - First pastor is called
1982 - Moved to bigger facilities
1984 - First pastor is forced to leave
1986 - Second pastor is called
1988 - Pastor sets new vision for the church
1990 - Church splits
1991 - Second pastor leaves for a new community

Action Step 2: Recall Significant Contributions to Your Growth and Decline

Take an 8½-by-14-inch sheet of paper, turn it lengthwise, and make five columns. Head them: PROBLEM, CONSEQUENCES, POSSIBLE SOLUTIONS, SUGGESTED IMPLEMENTATION, and TIME FRAME. As you identify a problem, put it in the left-hand column. You then need to correct whatever you can in order to reverse the process. Ask the Lord to show you His solution for each problem and the best steps for implementation, including His timetable. Put this information in the appropriate columns. Ask yourselves, "What happened?", "Why?", and "How did this affect prayer?"

Next, go back in the church's history to its founding. Write a brief description of why the church was founded. (Was it a Bible study that grew into a church, a church planted by a parent church, the result of a split from another church, etc.) Especially noteworthy is any negative basis for formation, such as a split. See figure 11 for a sample.

Figure 11

Significant Contributors to Growth and/or Decline

1977 - Founded for doctrinal purity and stand on separation

1978–82 - Forced to move to seven different facilities

1982 - Finds church facility for rent and signs lease for ten years

1984 - First pastor senses lack of support and is asked to leave

1986 - Second pastor is called, much younger than the first

1987 - Pastor challenges the church to evangelism

1988 - Vision statement is written and accepted by the congregation

1988 - Youth pastor is hired and young families start attending

1989 - Plans are introduced for a second hour of worship - Contemporary

1990 - Church splits

1991 - Second pastor is called to large ministry

Now, list all pastors (of any type), why they were called, and why they left. If available, check church attendance records. Make a graph showing the size of the church at each year from the time of founding. (See figure 12.) (Use number units appropriate to your size, such as increments of 10s, 50s, 100s, etc.) After making a line graph showing growth and decline, in the center, mark down at the appropriate period all known significant events in the church from inception such as building programs, move to new facilities, new pastor, church split, merge with another church, etc., graphing growth, plateau, and decline. Try to identify what contributed to the growth and decline.

Figure 12

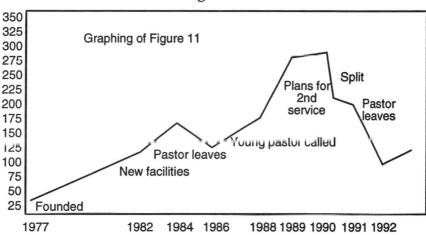

Action Step 3: Repent of the Past

Now that you have identified some of the "poison" that has caused you to lose heart and vision, start declining, and go into a dormant state, you are ready to ask the Lord to cleanse your church body of its sins and once again be a clean vessel for Him to fill and use.

Take the list of problems you compiled in Action Step 2. Ask the Lord to show you how to deal with each one. He may have you, as a leadership board, to go to anyone who has been offended or hurt by your church in the past. This would be especially true in the cases of splits and the rejection or removal of staff. You need to ask forgiveness for these acts even though the ones who were part of this sin may no longer be with the church. Still, just as Daniel identified with the sins of Israel and subsequently confessed them in the first person (9:4–11) (even though he probably had not participated personally in any of them), you, too, are responsible in the spiritual realm for the sins of your church fathers. (See also Exod. 34:7; Num. 14:18.)

By taking this step, you are releasing spiritually any rights the Enemy of our souls has had to keep your church weak and impotent. In essence, you are releasing the source of the sin and your resultant bondage or weakness.

Action Step 4: Release Wrong Patterns

Too often we can get into ruts in life and repeat wrong habits without even realizing it. Churches are as prone to this as are individuals. We tend to think, "Because we've never done this before, we can't do it now." Wrong! God wants us to grow. Growth indicates an expansion of what already exists and a healthy maintenance of the current body.

The child cannot be trusted to play with matches. But as he matures he can begin to use matches as he is trained to use them safely. Using this analogy with the church, you may have in the past tried something that God did not bless. You may have felt burned and therefore are resistant to ever trying it again. You know that others have been successful in doing what you are resisting, but you are not convinced your church should. Let God be the One to decide this issue. Go to Him, seek His guidance, and He will show you what He wants and will renew your church in ways you thought were impossible.

Small groups may be an area of ministry you've never tried in a formal way, or if you did, they soon fizzled out. Today, though, tremendous insights have been gained for success in this area. That's why you're reading this book, right? So commit to giving them a chance again (see Action Step 6).

Another area in which your church may need renewal may be in its resistance to changing times. You may have gotten stuck in the patterns of the '50s for worship, possibly because those in the decision-making positions of your congregation are of the older generation. But if you choose to stay outdated and do not reach out to the needs of the younger baby boomer and baby buster generations, you will almost inevitably doom yourself to losing this strategic segment of the church community.[2] You might keep people of your own age, who grew up in the church because of their love for your church, but you will not attract many others. We suggest you release this wrong view of worshiping and step fully into the beauty of worship in the '90s. This does not mean an either-or situation; it simply means adding some of the things like small groups and contemporary music, tastefully performed, that attract the younger people.

Action Step 5: Renew Your Commitment to Prayer

When your church first started, it is likely that much prayer saturated every aspect of ministry, every step taken. Why did it cool off? For it has, hasn't it? The Dormant Church is one that almost inevitably placed prayer at a more strategic level in the past, but presently prayer has either become a routine that never changes and has grown stale—almost like vain repetition—or it has faded out of the picture until it has become only a shadow of the powerful tool it once used to be.

So return to your first love. Repent for any prayerlessness. Ask the Lord to renew the heart you once had for prayer. Commit to placing prayer strategically at the heart of all you do and in every aspect of the church. We suggest you go through Action Steps 6 through 15 of *Power House*.[3] For individuals you will find that working through *Drawing Closer*[1] will help rekindle any flickering flame of relationship or weak prayer life. It will help sharpen your prayer skills and give you ways of identifying and eliminating hindrances to your prayer life and a close walk with the Lord.

Next, ask the Lord to show you what new opportunities He wants you to take advantage of in the areas of ministry. Let Him reveal any weak areas in your running of the church, and His solutions. Be open to the Spirit. When you are, God will increase your vision and renew your church in ways you thought were impossible.

Chapter 8 outlines steps to positioning prayer at the heart of your small groups.

Action Step 6: Recommit to Small Groups

Whether you called them small groups or not, you probably have had some all along: the Missionary Circles, Wednesday night prayer times, Bible studies in homes, Women's/Men's Fellowships, and similar regular gatherings. But we also can guess that as a Dormant Church these groups are not playing as vital a role as they once did or as they could because you have fallen into a routine. Too many churches did not lay the right foundation for their small groups or simply did not understand the dynamics involved in successful small groups. Their groups just evolved without real structure and thus suffered the natural consequences that come from lack of planning.

In chapter 8 we will go into more detail on how to avoid the pitfalls of small groups that die out after one to two years. We will show you how to keep them fresh and on the cutting edge as sharp ministry tools. So recommit to small groups. You will find they are being used by God in very significant ways to meet the needs of people living in the '90s.

Action Step 7: Revive Your Vision for the Great Commission

Lift up your eyes to your community. The fields are white unto harvest! Today more than ever, people need the Lord. Our society is desperate. Morality is almost nonexistent in many lives. "Self has been exalted and people are living empty lives of quiet desperation," as one cynic rightly put it.

The Lord has established your church in a unique position within your community. He has plans for you to touch the lives in your area. Ask Him to show you these plans, to increase your vision, and to give you His heart for these people whom Jesus loves and wants to be part of His body.

There are many great ministry tools to help you do this, including Evangelism Explosion, The Four Spiritual Laws, and The JESUS Video Project (an evangelistic plan to saturate your community with the video *JESUS*.[5] In some cities you can do this in cooperation with other churches).

Action Step 8: Reevaluate Where Small Groups Fit into the Church

Small groups can be used in so many areas, covering a multitude of subjects. We will be looking at some of these ways in following chapters, especially chapters 8 and 9. You will find that small groups can form a solid foundation for almost any ministry. For example, your youth group can have its regular meetings, then, where appropriate, have smaller home Bible study and fellowship times throughout the week. You may want to look at having prayer groups, both large and small. Some of these can be prayer only; others can divide between significant prayer time and Bible study. The large groups can be focused on a specific ministry area such as missionaries; the men who have attended Promise Keepers; a women's or men's breakfast; early morning prayer times at the church; a retired group meeting for Bible study; prayer and then fellowship or an outing; recovery groups of different types: groups for singles, older singles, young marrieds, divorced, divorced and remarried, as well as single parents. These are just a few ways small groups can be structured to enhance the ministry of the church and to develop more unity and bonding to the church and to each other. Recommitting to small groups can be a strong step toward emerging from your dormant state and advancing to the next level of church growth.

Action Step 9: Revitalize the Church's Focus

In life, we talk about the need to revitalize our lives as we grow older. We take vitamins and supplements to increase our energy levels. We buy expensive creams to revitalize our skin. We exercise and in general try to reverse the natural tendency to deteriorate as the aging process speeds up. If we don't take such steps, we will usually suffer down the line as our life expectancy is shortened by physical problems. At best, our quality of life and our appearance will suffer if we do not take the necessary steps to revitalize ourselves.

Our churches suffer the same need for revitalization. That is ever so true of the Dormant Church. Most churches that fall into this classification are in desperate need of a "Body Revitalization Program."

The above action steps are part of the body program. Another part of your church body you will need to improve is its vision and goals. How is your vision? Do you need new spiritual glasses? What about that long-distance vision you had for goals? Is it still sharp? The goals you've had for your church may or may not need to be adjusted and updated. An educated guess would conclude that virtually all Dormant Churches can benefit from analyzing the current focus of the church and then prayerfully updating it. Goals are important, and we strive for them. But some churches do not set new ones once they reach a given set of goals. Other churches may have goals, but as leadership changes, these goals fall by the wayside and are forgotten. Too many Dormant Churches exist because they've been around so long that they don't know how to stop existing. The Lord was very definite when He warned us that without a vision, we perish (Prov. 29:18). Vision can provide that spark of life that will energize the whole body to start the renewal process. Revitalize your goals, cast a new vision, and watch the Lord put new life, meaning, and purpose into your body. Your people should be excited about their church. Vision and goals are keys to creating such an atmosphere.

The Dormant Church is much loved by the Lord. But He loves you too much to let you remain where you are. We are convinced that if you follow carefully the Action Steps, along with any other things the Lord shows you, there is no way yours will remain a Dormant Church. Restoration, revitalization, and renewal will result as your church returns to God's wonderful plan and fulfills all the good works He has for your church to accomplish in the lives of your members and in the community in which He planted you.

CHAPTER SEVEN

The Dedicated Church

John Claypool tells a great parable about the Christian life. It's a story about a peasant who lived in a village at the foot of a mountain range. On the side of the mountain, in full view of the village, stood a monastery. The village people seldom saw any of the monks, but they held them in high esteem.

One day a monk descended from the mountain to the village below. A peasant, running up to the monk, said, "Oh, Father, surely yours is the best of all lives, living so close to God up in the clouds on top of the mountain. Please tell me, what do you do up there?"

After a thoughtful pause, the monk replied, "What do we do up there? Well, I'll tell you. We fall down, and we get up. We fall down, and we get up. We fall down, and we get up."[1]

Falling down and getting up is a picture of the Christian life. We are all a part of the "Skinned Knees Club." As each of us progresses in the Christian life, we fall down and constantly need to get back up with God's help.

Churches grow in a similar fashion. A church does not grow on a steady incline but moves forward through cycles of growth, plateau, decline, and renewed growth. When a church finds itself on a plateau or in a period of decline, it has the option of remaining there or getting back up and moving forward with renewed energy. Churches in the category of a Dedicated Church often are either on a spiritual plateau or just beginning to slip into decline. They need to restore their vision for the future before they can effectively employ a small group ministry.

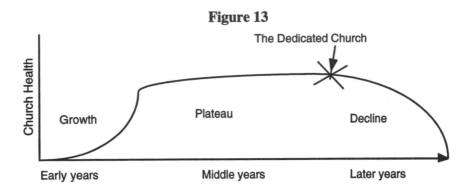

Figure 13

The Key to Health: Renewal of the Vision

Renewing a sense of vision is the key to preparing the Dedicated Church for a small group ministry. George Barna defines vision as "a clear mental image of a preferable future imparted by God to His chosen servants and is based upon an accurate understanding of God, self and circumstances."[2] Oftentimes church leaders think it is up to them to create a vision. This thinking is inaccurate, and it places the burden in the wrong place. Note the phrase, "imparted by God" in Barna's definition. It is God who creates the vision. Our job is to discover the vision He already has for our church.

There are three questions to ask while searching for God's vision: *What* does God want our church to accomplish? *How* does He want it achieved? And, *when* does He wish it to be consummated? The *what* usually comes as your church members and leaders specifically ask God to show them His vision for their church. Investigating the needs of the unchurched community and your people's ability to address those needs informs the prayers of the church. Over a period of time a passion grows that God is calling the church to achieve something great for His kingdom. When the specifics of this passion are written down, it becomes the corporate vision of the church.

The *how* grows out of the corporate vision and is determined by the skills, gifts, and abilities of your people. Many times the *how* develops over time and is different from original expectations. The people of Israel did not expect the exodus to last forty years. In the most famous Holy Land trip ever recorded, a projected week-long journey turned into a forty-year excursion in the desert. The *how* was much different from what the people anticipated. Gideon never perceived that the *how* of winning a major battle was to narrow his army down to three hundred men. Likewise, as your church develops a strategy to fulfill God's vision, seek to remain open and flexible so that God can direct you in His way.

Once God shows your church the *what* and the *how*, the next insight is the *when*. Too often church leaders ask God to bless what they are doing. In contrast, effective churches ask, "Lord, give us the wisdom to see what You are already blessing." One growing church used the following as its purpose statement: "Find out what God is doing and get on board." Ultimately God's vision is right before our eyes. Look around your city. What is God obviously blessing? How could you get on board with God and take part in His vision?

As you seek God in prayer for His vision for your church, keep in mind the following ideas.

Develop Enthusiasm for Outreach

The word *enthusiasm* comes from two Greek words, *en* and *theos*, meaning "in God." If a church is truly "in God," it cannot help but be excited about the work of God. Godly enthusiasm is a vital force within any church. A Dedicated Church may look like it is healthy on the surface. Its ministries may function well, people may be cared for, and money may be sent to foreign fields. If it has lost its enthusiasm for reaching the lost, however, then its vitality is gradually draining away.

Do the leaders of your church have a passion for reaching the lost? At the core of God's work is His program of redemption. To seek God's vision for your church is to be enthusiastic about what excites the heart of God. To renew a passion for the lost among your people, consider a preaching series on "How to Care for the Unchurched." Have your church members list the names of their unchurched friends, family members, and daily acquaintances and then ask them to commit to a year of prayer for those on their lists. As appropriate, share your own concern for the lost, and highlight the passion of others for bringing friends to Christ. Remember: What you talk about most to your people becomes the church's vision over time.

Dream Big

Since God is a big God, we should expect that His vision will stretch our church beyond its normal expectations. God is always stretching us, causing us to walk more and more by faith. Jesus' whole life seemed to be one of teaching people to live by faith, especially the disciples. His harshest words dealt with their lack of faith: "You of little faith" (Matt. 16:8). "How long shall I stay with you and put up with you?" (Luke 9:41, after the disciples could not heal the boy with an evil spirit). So, when you establish goals, let the Lord help you dream big dreams. Then you will have the joy of seeing what He can do in and through you. Your capacity to be used by Him will be enlarged as you become a sharper instrument in His hands because you have allowed Him to stretch you and mold you in a seemingly impossible yet successful undertaking. Paul experienced this when he proclaimed the paradox, "When I am weak, then I am strong" (2 Cor. 12:10b). He knew the reality of having before him goals that only God could accomplish.

Be Sensitive to God's Timing

When we get in a hurry, we can make silly mistakes. Abraham and Sarah knew God's will for them was to have a baby. Their problems came when they didn't wait for His timing. After years of waiting to see the child of promise, they took matters into their own hands by saying, "God, we know what You want. So we'll help You." Nowhere do we read of them consulting God on His possible solution to their waiting game. So they created a mess, which God to this day is having to clean up. But He let them proceed, and in turn they, and hopefully we, learned from their mistake. The mistake did not disqualify them for God's eventual fulfillment of His promise; it only complicated their lives when *His* child of promise was finally born. The bottom line is: ask, listen, and then wait for God's timing.

Focus on God's Values

Values are the basic concepts or beliefs of a church. Some will be written down, but most are unwritten. A good exercise for your leaders is to attempt to list the hidden values that drive their decision making. At your next board meeting, ask your leaders to share what they think are the crucial values of your church. Write them on an overhead projector or chalkboard for everyone to see. Over the next year refine your list by adding or subtracting from it until you have a clear understanding of what your church values the most.[3]

Values are the priorities of your church. They establish the grid by which you make decisions. Therefore it is vital to the health of your church that your values reflect the values of God. We make a mistake when we set our values based upon human reasoning. Therefore, when developing your vision, be certain your values line up with Scripture and that you have consulted the Lord for His desires in whatever you are doing.

Redefine Success

We tend to define success or failure based upon what man (including ourselves) thinks about our performance. But for the Christian, success and failure should be defined by what God thinks about our performance. His standard is for us to live up to the mark He sets for us, not what we or others set for us. For example, we think in terms of numbers as being a success or failure. Yet, God's orientation is toward the heart of the individual. Gideon's army demonstrates how God works in different ways. Gideon wanted an army—God wanted wise men. David sinned when he depended upon how many soldiers he had rather than depending on the God who would lead him into battle. His heart was not right, so he failed. Even Jesus pared down the number of His followers by eliminating all but twelve from His close companions. Given the fact that once He left earth, only those He had trained would be used to reach the world, one would naturally think that the more who were trained, the better. But it was the heart of men that mattered to Him, not the outward image. So define your successes and failures by God's standards.

Evaluate Properly

The Lord should be the One evaluating all we do. He needs to tell us how well we are doing and what changes we should make. After all, it is His ministry. He was the One who initiated in your heart the desire to start a small group ministry. He is the One who therefore can best tell you your effectiveness. Resist comparing yourself with a church that isn't doing as well as yours, as it doesn't take long to get prideful. The opposite is also a trap. If you compare yourself to a church that's doing better than yours is, you could easily slip into depression. Paul learned this lesson. He wrote to the Corinthian Christians: "I care very little if I am judged by you or by any human court; indeed, I do not even judge myself" (1 Cor. 4:3). He goes on to write in verse 4 that instead he let the Holy Spirit do the judging. This is a lesson we all need to learn and apply.

Develop Leaders

Healthy churches identify, train, and deploy leaders to grow as a team. Volunteers must take ownership of the vision, help further it, enhance it, expand it, and be the hands, feet, and mouths to implement it. There is only a certain amount any leader can accomplish alone. Thus, developing other leaders is a necessary aspect of fulfilling God's vision for your church. According to Bill Hybels, "Leaders are not users of people. Leaders are those who cast a vision until they find those who want to join with that vision. Then the leader commits to developing that person while together they achieve their dream."[4]

If your church is in the category of a Dedicated Church, you have to renew your vision and faith. Without the people of your church, you will never be all that God wants you to be. So step back for a minute. Look at your church with honest candor. How is your vision? Can you see clearly what God wants to do with small groups in your church? Are you willing to step out in faith even though you will have to deal with the inevitable bumps along the way? Do certain potential problems intimidate you too much? Are you at the point of saying, "I just can't stand any more criticism. My plate is full, and I am wearing out"? If these statements describe you, you need to ask the Lord for a fresh vision. God says, "Where there is no revelation, the people cast off restraint" (Prov. 29:18, NIV).This lack of vision may be why you are withering on a plateau or sliding down the slope of decline. Request a renewal of your faith. Ask for His help to meet head-on whatever problems may come. Push through those barriers of resistance that may be holding you back.

Remember, in the long run the results will be worth the effort because you will have allowed God to work through you to accomplish in people's lives what otherwise would never have happened. As you are pursuing God's vision, discouragement can often pull you down. This is when you need to trust in God. When you trust Him, you can conquer your problems and your discouragement because you know you are part of God's greater plan.

CHAPTER EIGHT

The Developing Church

When Apple Computer fell on difficult days a while back, Apple's young chairman, Steven Jobs, traveled from the Silicon Valley to New York City. His purpose was to convince Pepsico's John Sculley to move west and run his struggling company. As the two men overlooked the Manhattan skyline from Sculley's penthouse office, the Pepsi executive started to decline Jobs's offer.

Sculley told him that he would want a million-dollar salary, a million-dollar bonus, and a million-dollar severance pay. Jobs was shocked, but agreed to the terms on the condition that Sculley would move to California. Still Sculley would only commit to being a consultant from New York. At that moment in the negotiation, Jobs issued a challenge. He said, "Do you want to spend the rest of your life selling sugared water, or do you want to change the world?"

In Sculley's autobiography, he admits that this challenge knocked the wind out of him. He wrote that he had become so caught up in the future of Pepsi, his pension, and whether his family could adapt to life in California that an opportunity to "change the world" nearly passed him by. Instead, he stepped back, put his life in perspective, and went to Apple.

Many churches do not recognize the chance to change the world. The Developing Church, however, has the will and the skill to make a difference in its world by creating community.

Staying Involved

Making a difference through the church requires faith and active involvement. The Developing Church models such faith and activity.

The Developing Church emphasizes staying involved in personal growth in Christ. The Christian walk begins when a person places his or her faith in Jesus, but we are also exhorted to grow in our faith. "Yeah, but I'm just kinda coasting right now." Never forget that coasting only happens when a person is going downhill. The standard God has set for our Christian life is to grow in faith and in understanding of the Scriptures. We are told in 2 Timothy 3:15–17, "You have known the holy Scriptures, which are able to make you wise for salvation through faith in Christ Jesus. All Scripture is God-breathed and is useful for teaching, rebuking, correcting and training in righteousness, so that the man of God may be thoroughly equipped for every good work."

The Developing Church emphasizes staying involved in the building up of the family. In the Old Testament times, the extended family often had the grandparents living in the home or very close by. They helped in many ways such as baby-sitting and giving advice. Today, with our fast-paced lives and our desire to be free of our relatives and live independent of them and they of us, we have lost the dynamic and benefit the extended family offered. Therefore, with so much isolation in our world, families need support and encouragement.

Paul showed us how the church can play a significant role in meeting this need for support. We are to instruct one another with the godly wisdom we have learned (Rom. 15:14; 1 Cor. 1:5; Col. 3:16). The older women are to teach the younger, as he spelled out in Titus 2:3b–5: "[older women are] to teach what is good. Then they can train the younger women to love their husbands and children, to be self-controlled and pure, to be busy at home, to be kind, and to be subject to their husbands, so that no one will malign the word of God." This is a type of mentoring. Also, in Ephesians 5 and 6 Paul provided the church with guidelines to help the church instruct family members on how to relate to one another and to the Lord. Fathers are exhorted not to exasperate their children but instead to bring them up in the training and instruction of the Lord (6:4). Children are told to obey their parents (6:1). Chapter 5 gives instructions on how husbands and wives are to respond to each other (5:22–25. See also 1 Pet. 3).

Developing Churches emphasize staying involved in evangelism. Peter emphasizes for us the importance of being ready to share the gospel, "But in your hearts set apart Christ as Lord. Always be prepared to give an answer to everyone who asks you to give the reason for the hope that you have" (1 Pet. 3:15). But how? Discipleship. And who should know more about discipleship than the one who was personally discipled by Jesus in two small groups (the twelve and the inner circle of three). Small groups offer that easy way to teach biblical knowledge in a pleasant setting. The very fact that others are there to learn from helps stimulate a person's desire to learn. Also, as people share their faith, they will find gaps in their knowledge, which will cause them to want to know more. This desire for more knowledge may create the need for a new small group—one on witnessing or on some of the cults, such as Jehovah's Witnesses and Mormons.

Lastly, Developing Churches stay involved in what God is doing. They do not pray, "Lord bless what we are doing." Instead their prayer is, "Lord, we want to do what You are blessing." Jesus, who is our model of how to live the Christian life, operated at this level. He explained how it works in John 5:19: "I tell you the truth, the Son can do nothing by himself; he can do only what he sees his Father doing, because whatever the Father does the Son also does."

The Key to Health: Renewed Commitment

For those of you who are married, remember how it was when you found you were madly in love with the one who would one day be your spouse? You found life unbearable without this wonderful person. So you took the step, got engaged, and set the date. Remember the way you felt about each other on your wedding day? What a deep level of commitment you had to your life together and to making your marriage work.

But as time passed, inevitably that commitment was challenged, stretched, and even strained as problems and frustrations occurred that you never dreamed of at the beginning. Without solid, unwavering commitment to each other, you easily could have thrown in the towel, split, and been remarried by now with a brand-new set of problems!

As Christians we are in a similar position. We came to Jesus with our hearts broken over our sins, but full of love and rejoicing for His provision to deal with our sin. We took the step, committed to Him, and started a new life together with Him. But for many, the intensity of their first love has faded. Their commitment has vanished, and they find themselves following a routine instead of a relationship. Unfortunately this can also be true for the local church. No church starts off lukewarm. Each church always starts off with great vision and desire to be what God wants it to be. The members set goals and pour their lives into reaching those goals and becoming a successful church. But too many members lose the sharp edge of their first love and need to come to a time of recommitment in order to be all God wants them to be as a church. They need to go back to Him, ask Him for His plans for them, and then implement all He shows them to do. For most congregations, small groups of one type or another likely will be a central ingredient in God's plans for strengthening commitment in the local church.

Seven Keys to Starting Small Groups in the Developing Church

The small group is such an important element of the Developing Church. You will want to get yours started on a solid foundation with the proper perspective and motives for initiating and running your groups. The following seven keys will be helpful in identifying fundamental principles for success with small groups.

Key 1: Commit Totally to the Concept of Small Group Ministry

Experience is showing how vital small groups are to the heart of the church of the '90s. Therefore you must do, with the Lord's leading, whatever it takes to succeed.

The Lord says that whatever we do, we are to do it with all our heart. In fact, in Luke 9:62 Jesus clearly states that we are not to do things halfway or plan to turn back. "No one who puts his hand to the plow and looks back is fit for service in the kingdom of God." When we commit to something and say, "We'll try it for a while and see how it goes," our level of commitment and enthusiasm is not high enough to create and then sustain the energy to bring success to the effort. You need to be convinced that this is what God wants and that with His help and guidance, your small group will succeed. God does not lead us into failures. We are not convinced of His leading when we say we might fail. If this is our attitude, then we will be operating in our own power and strength—not a good way to work! Jesus is in our boat, and He has said to us, "Let's go to the other side," not "Let's go and see how things work out, for we can always return if we want." Confidence in our ability to hear from the Lord can be undermined in our people if we operate on anything other than full steam ahead.

Key 2: Continue Training

Small groups need attention periodically to be most effective. You can't just set them up as a healthy body, let them go, and expect them to thrive. They need monitoring, evaluation, and continued training. Why more training? Because topics change, leadership may change as people move away or want to take a furlough, and new groups may need to be formed. Therefore you will always want to have people in training so they can step in at a moment's notice when the need arises. In addition, this gives you people to use when you may need them for other positions in the church, such as Sunday school classes, AWANA, or Vacation Bible School. It also gives you qualified people to fill in for vacationing leaders.

You will want to mentor your people in the following key areas:

Follow-up Skills. A good teacher knows how to keep in touch with those who are part of her group. Teach your people how to be sensitive to the needs of group members and how to pick up on signs of problems or when a person is not sharing his or her heart, but only what they think you want to hear. Reviewing body language will be helpful. Assist potential teachers to establish rapport and maintain a good relationship with their group members. Help them to have an accurate understanding about where each person is and then to know how to help the members of the group go from where they are to where God wants them to be.

How to Properly Study the Bible. You can use different methods in order to gain the most from Bible study. You need to know that your aspiring leaders know the best methods available to do this. You will want to familiarize them with the appropriate study helps including concordances, topical Bibles, and commentaries.

Leading in Prayer. This is a skill that does not come easily for many because too often they have never seen it modeled. Your followers need to know that leading prayer is a learned skill; the Lord will help them with it; and it will become easier as they practice it. Model for them and the group the fact that prayers do not have to be long or eloquent. Prayers are better when you offer them from your heart to the Lord's heart. Remind them that their public prayers will reflect both their own private prayer lives and their individual walks with the Lord. When they have sin in their lives, their prayers may reveal this. Encourage them to keep short accounts with the Lord.

You can use seven types of prayer in small groups. Suggest that everyone listen and agree silently or softly with what is being prayed. Do not use the prayer time to think up your own wording for your prayers. You will notice that some of these types of prayers are most appropriate for personal prayer time at home. We need to stretch people in their prayer skills.

During your small group meeting you may want to use a variety of prayer styles. The most common way to pray as a group is to have everyone praying as one person leads (either the leader or a group member). But you can also break up into twos, threes, and so forth.

1. *Topical.* Topical prayer can cover such areas as the staff; church interest; the local, state, and federal governments; or current issues that affect members. One subject or many subjects can be covered, as guided by the leader.

2. *Conversational.* Conversational prayer should be offered in short segments with random subjects. Suggest that no one move to a new subject until those who want to pray for the first one have had an opportunity to do so.

3. *Applicable.* Have the member of the group pray that they will apply to their lives the lessons they learned in the study.

4. *Expressional.* A rewarding type of prayer can be offered to God in written form. Give the participants time to write a love letter to God or make a list of things they have to thank God for. Those who feel comfortable may want to read their prayer to the group. This can be very touching as see the heart of the individual. They also may see some new ways of expressing their own thoughts to the Lord. Let them know that it may take a while to develop this skill. Encourage the members who like this style of prayer to continue using it at home.

5. *Transferrable.* Using a preset pattern for prayer can be helpful in giving guidelines for prayer, both within the group and privately. Examples might be using the different elements of the Lord's Prayer or the ACTS acrostic (Adoration, Confession, Thanksgiving, Supplication).

6. *Meditational.* Prayer involves listening as well as speaking. However, with the busyness of today's society, sometimes it is hard to be silent before the Lord and listen to Him. But silent meditation is a way of praying that brings its own rewards and is worth the time it

takes to learn how to do it. Remind your people that they may not feel comfortable being silent before the Lord at first, but as with any new skill, as they keep up the effort, they will reap the results, and it will become easier.

7. *Relational.* It is encouraging to pray with others. We suggest you have the members of your group form permanent prayer partners with whom they can pray during the week. Another way to connect with others during the small group time is to ask people for requests and then ask for a volunteer to pray for the request. You may also want to suggest that the group members pray for this request throughout the week as the Lord brings it to mind. Another relational method is to break up into small groups and have each person share a request. Then either have volunteers pray for the request, have the person to the left or right of the person pray for the request, or have everyone pray for it.

One very popular type of relational prayer is called prayer triplets. To do this, divide the group into units of three. Each person lists on a three-by-five-inch card five unsaved friends or relatives for whom they would like prayer in the coming days. They make two of these cards to give to the other two group members. Then each person has fifteen names to be praying for concerning salvation. As people are saved, they add new names to the list. This is a very relational way to pray for the concerns of each other.

Handling Criticism Well. People do not like it when others disagree with or criticize them. Unfortunately, small groups are not immune from having people voice differing opinions. In fact, we want our participants to feel free to express their views and their understanding of the subject but in a positive way. You need to help those you mentor learn tactful ways to handle dissenting opinions. It is also important to help them distinguish when a wrong answer needs to be exposed.

Our rule of thumb is to correct mistakes only if *not* to do so would bring a damaging wrong point of view to the group that could not be identified by everyone as error. For example, it would be necessary to say what is true about the Trinity, but it would not be necessary to insist on your point of view about the literal six days of creation versus one day being as a thousand years to the Lord.

Sometimes one way around the gray areas is to say, "Some people hold your point of view. Let me share what mine is and why I have chosen to view it this way." Addressing the less volatile questions in this manner will keep you from having to be dogmatic but will still convey which view you believe so the participants can have some guidelines in areas that are not black and white.

Discouragement. Discouragement is always ready to rear its ugly head if we give it half a chance. Things can be going well and all of a sudden a bump appears in the road—someone joins the group who doesn't fit in or gives trouble; a negative discussion occurs; circumstances change that bring added pressure; people don't respond as anticipated; attendance starts to drop. These are just a few of the sources that can open up the door to discouragement. You need to train your people ahead of time on how to minimize these problems in the first place, and then how best to deal with each one if they appear.

Fatigue and burnout can also become fertile ground for discouragement. Things always look black when we are tired. This often will be the case when financial, medical, interpersonal, or other problems have us under pressures before we step into our small group setting.

Therefore, it is important to emphasize three things:

1. Know what God's will is, that is, know that He wants this small group.

2. Look ahead to see where problems might come, and avoid them.

3. Trust the Lord to solve the problems, and don't look at the problem without seeing the Lord and His solution in it.

Leadership Skills. Those you mentor need to learn how to be leaders whom people will follow. Some you choose may be natural leaders; others won't be. But often even the natural leader needs some guidelines as to how to lead in a Christian context. All will learn from you but will need to hear specific teaching on how to be good, godly leaders. Giving them books to read or tapes to listen to will help bring them up to better standards. Having discussions on different problems, even role-playing as a group, can be useful. And who knows, you may learn some new skills yourself!

Discussion Leading. The heart of any good small group is the time of discussion. That is why you need to mentor well your aspiring leaders to know how to lead a discussion. Some of the skills a good discussion leader needs include:

- Knowing how to ask questions that are open-ended and need interaction rather than a single yes or no response.
- Having balance between teaching and interaction so as not to dominate the process. Usually the more good interaction you can stimulate, the better.
- Being willing to say "I don't know, but I'll find out," instead of faking your way through with some type of answer that won't be accurate or is unsatisfying.
- Learning how to draw people into the discussion. This includes being sensitive to who is answering, who may know the next answer, and not embarrassing a person who is too timid to respond at first.
- Being able to recognize and steer around problem areas.
- How not to feel threatened by different opinions.
- How to anticipate possible questions and problem areas. Preferably, you need to know how to plan to stop them before they arise or at least how to handle them if they do arise.

As part of teaching the above skills, you might want to consider meeting regularly with those you are mentoring to go over what they observed in the group time. This will help you point out to them things you were doing that they might have missed but will surely see the next time around because of this discussion. It also can be a learning time for you, as they often give valuable insights you might have missed. These are times when iron sharpens iron.

Key 3: Create Opportunities

You can use many different types of groupings for Bible studies:
- Recovery groups (We tend to lump everything into one here and deal with principles. We can apply the specifics as a person asks or as we see a need to talk about a specific addiction.)
- Service groups (missionary, Union Rescue Mission, social issues, etc.)
- Study groups (for men, women, and couples)
- Bible study groups
- Topical groups (on parenting, empty nesters, aging, grief, etc.)
- Support groups (single parents, divorced and remarrieds)
- Prayer groups
- Care groups
- Single groups
- Newlywed groups

The more opportunities and variety you offer, the better the chances of getting more people involved. Two notes of warning, though. Be certain that each group has a strong biblical basis. For example, recovery groups can get off base by seeing self-effort as the focus rather than turning your weakness over to the Lord for Him to help you solve your problems. Other similar groups can degenerate into complaint or "Here's what I did" groups that can drift away from biblical moorings and end up being nothing more than focus groups you could find in any secular setting.

The other warning is to be certain you don't just throw out Scripture as the solution to a problem, but rather show *how* this Scripture can be *applied*. This pratical application may require a sample prayer or some role-playing to help bring the point home.

Key 4: Compile Data

To best serve your people, it is helpful to know as much as possible about them in a number of categories. One way is to ask yourself, *How is assimilation in our church doing?* You can determine this through the percent of visitors retained and the percent of people in small groups. Also survey the church members for appropriate small group topics. You may want to suggest some topics and let them add to your list.

After you have compiled this information you will then want to determine the types of groups needed (parents, seniors, business, college, young couples without kids, divorced, divorced and remarried, etc.), and the percent of parents who need child care and when.

From this data you will have a clearer picture of where the church is and what areas need work.

Key 5: Connect with Other Churches

The church is a body, and the body needs to communicate in order to be its strongest. The old question "Why reinvent the wheel?" is appropriate for the small group setting. Check with other churches to find out what they're doing that works. Evaluate their small group programs in order to determine whether some of the things they are doing or a modification of them will work for your church. Ask them for input on areas in which you are struggling or having a problem. They may also be able to recommend some good resources.

Next, find out what other churches are doing that doesn't work. Certainly you will want to avoid their mistakes.

Finally, pool ideas. You may want to do some joint things with them in the future.

Key 6: Covenant for the Long Haul

One mistake often made in forming a group is having a great subject but not setting goals or a time frame for the group. We will cover this in more detail in chapter 13. There we indicate that most groups will last only one and a half to two years if you do not have an ending date. Therefore, to get the maximum benefit and keep interest high, you need to have an ending date. As we also noted, this time period may be as long as nine months or as short as three months. At the end of a period you can always decide to go on, but there again, set a new ending time. With today's mentality, setting limits works best. When you follow this rule of thumb, you will find your people will stay with you for the long haul with few dropping out along the way.

It is also important to set goals. Here are some questions to consider as you set goals:

How long will you be their pastor? You don't want to start a new program if you plan on leaving in the foreseeable future and will not be able to give the proper guidance and oversight to the small groups. Even if you are delegating most of the responsibilities, your leaving can cause a drop in attendance because of the disappointment and adjustments that will result.

How many are ready to participate? You need to have people and resources to work with as you start small groups—homes that will be open (or places at church), leaders to take on some of the groups, people to train, and so forth. The Lord wants us to do things decently and in order, so until you have the people in place, don't begin your small groups. However, if you know the Lord is leading you to start such groups, know also that He assumes the responsibility to show you those He wants involved. They will be there, but you may have to seek His face to discover who they are.

What are your abilities and gifts? You may be gifted to lead the small groups, especially if you have no visible leaders waiting in the wings and must train people. But hopefully you will have leaders ready and eager to take over the reins after you give the program its initial start.

Key 7: Concentrate on Integration

You will be most successful if you focus on integrating small groups into every area of ministry. Small groups become the backbone, the foundation from which you build each ministry. They are like glue that helps keep people interested and participating in whatever ministries your church offers. For example, do you want to do evangelism? How about having a small group study the Book of Acts, and incorporate witnessing as part of the homework assignment, praying for three to five lost friends as a part of the prayer within the group and at home. You could also include praying for the unsaved friends of your prayer partner and others within the group.

Small groups can be exciting when they are done right. For the Developing Church they can be a strong tool to help in many different areas of ministry. They provide a way of meeting needs in creative ways, of establishing unity and strong bonds to the church. Small groups provide a natural source of new leaders who are properly mentored. Jesus used small groups to eventually reach the world. When done right, your small groups can and will help you to disciple your people to a deeper level, and in turn to reach out in evangelistic ways to the community in which God has placed your church.

CHAPTER NINE

The Dynamic Church

We are both sports fanatics. We love to watch sports and even when the ego allows, get involved in a few pickup games. Enjoying the sports world has caused us to be acutely aware of stories involving the great motivators of our era. One such story involves the legendary head coach of the Green Bay Packers as he enjoyed his last season coaching football.

Certainly those who worked for Vince Lombardi respected his work, his love for the game, and his loyalty to the players. On one occasion, Lombardi's team had suffered a humiliating defeat. Standing before his team, there was little he could say because these men were professionals who recognized the faults and the lack of practice in certain areas that had caused the defeat. The members of his football team understood that they had not played well and that they had not stayed with the game plan.

Lombardi was a dynamic leader and understood the fundamentals of leadership. In his quiet, assertive style he reached down and picked up a football. He then smiled at the men and shared five words: "Men, this is a football." Obviously, Lombardi was attempting to get back to the basics, and one of his men in particular understood their dire need to review the essentials. At the appropriate moment this man raised his hand and said, "Hold on, Coach, you're going too fast!"

The Dynamic Church is one that has reviewed the basics, understands the basics, and puts the basics into practice. But Lombardi and his team recognized that there was still one key for the victory they desired to become a reality and that key was prepared leadership.

The Key to Health: Prepared Leadership

In the *Last Days Newsletter*, Leonard Ravenhill tells about a group of tourists who were visiting a picturesque village. They walked by an old man sitting beside a fence. In a rather patronizing way, one tourist asked, "Were any great men born in this village?" To which the old man replied, "Nope, only babies."[1]

A frothy question brought a very profound answer. There are no instant heroes, whether in this world or in the kingdom of God. Growth takes time and spiritual leadership must be earned. We have designed a very simple acrostic to describe the kind of preparedness that is necessary for leading the Dynamic Church and building a system of community within its body. A leader must be P.R.E.P.A.R.E.D.

A Leader Must Have PURPOSE and Direction

It is hard to lead if you do not know where you are going. The leader must know the purpose for the group and understand where he wants to lead them. This requires seeking the Lord so He can show the direction for the group. Then in turn the leader needs to communicate this purpose and vision to the group members so they will want to be a continuing part of the team.

A Leader Must Demonstrate RESPONSIBILITY to the Team

A team is just that—a group of individuals who work together. There are no lone rangers, no person who can do it all by himself. The quarterback has to prepare himself to be the best quarterback possible. He has to memorize the plays, know when to use them, and try to figure out the enemy's game plan. So it is with our small groups. The "quarterback leader" has a high degree of responsibility to the group to be prepared, to transfer his knowledge skillfully to the needs of the group members so they can perform well too. It is sad to see a leader who is not prepared, who is late, or who in general displays a lack of enthusiasm for the small group or the people in it.

A Leader Must Desire EXCELLENCE in His Life

Any leader is a role model, especially in the church. Therefore church leaders have a high responsibility before the Lord, for they have been given much and therefore much will be required of them (Luke 12:48). They have a mandate from the Lord to do whatever they do with excellence (1 Cor. 14:12; Col. 3:5–17). They need to model the fruit of the Spirit (Gal. 5:22–23). If they come poorly prepared or are not enthusiastic about their ministry, it will show, and the group will be affected by their attitude. Whatever we do for the Lord has to be of the best quality. He deserves nothing less than our best. Our small group members deserve the best too.

A Leader Must Remain PERSISTENT toward His Goals

Paul had goals that he pressed toward. We need to have the same. That means we are determined to reach those goals and nothing is going to stop us—not our fatigue or our overworked bodies. No obstacles or problems of any kind will be allowed by the dedicated, persistent leader to stop him from reaching the goal the Lord has placed before him. Just as the disciples should have known when Jesus got in the boat and said they were going to the other side that no obstacle could stop them, so believers today have a rich scriptural model to follow of men and women who have been persistent leaders for the Lord.

For example, once David was crowned king, even though it took many long years of struggle and danger before he sat on the throne, still he persisted and never gave up. In more recent history, this was the attitude of Sir Winston Churchill when he told a group of graduates that the key to success is, "Never give up! Never, never, never, never give up!" Such determination and persistence needs to be at the heart of each small group leader if he is to succeed. It will not always be a proverbial bed of roses, especially if you are to be the leader of a group God will touch. You can know that the Enemy will do all he can to stop your success. That is why you need to be determined and persistent with God's help to reach your goals for the group. Only then will you be able to overcome whatever obstacles you encounter.

A Leader Must Demonstrate ATTENTION to Details

Not every leader has the innate ability to follow through on every detail for every occasion. But a prepared leader will demonstrate a desire to be consistent in their administrative follow-up. We are seeing a tremendous move of God in today's churches toward empowerment of leaders. Paul shared in Ephesians 4 that pastors are called to equip saints, to be involved and share the work load so that the body of Christ is built up. In a team orientation, where leadership is genuinely prepared for the tasks before them, everyone has the responsibility traditionally given to the leader. Thus, in demonstrating an attention to details, problems and ideas are all shared. Differences are respected and growth and development are the goals. It is not enough for the "top guns" of the church to follow through. Some of the details which will be of primary concern will be the reporting structure to the leadership, for both blessings and difficulties; pastoral care where needed; continuing education; follow-up of new-comers; curriculum research; and all the details simply associated with meeting places, beverages, and the like. Prepared leaders move beyond reactivity into proactivity and resolve these kinds of issues as they arise.

A Leader Must Have a RESOLVE to Contribute

It is possible that many of your leaders will not be driven, type-A personalities. Therefore, they will need to overcome the normal desire to maintain the status quo or to let someone else do the job. They will need to see that God has selected them to do this job, and they must resolve to do it no matter how they feel about it. Thus each person you challenge to a position of small group leadership must pray about it first. They must take ownership for the call and then resolve to do whatever the Lord shows them. Only in this way will your leader remain solid and unwavering from the call of God on their lives.

A Leader Must Put Forth an EFFORT

It almost goes without saying. Small group leaders will need to expend a lot of effort. Leading a group is not something they can do off the cuff because they have a gift of teaching or of gab. They will need to spend time praying and seeking the Lord, preparing the lessons, mentoring, and listening to and praying for people, just to mention a few of the responsibilities.

A Leader Must Be DEVOTED to the People

Sadly, some people lead only because they are gifted and because they love and want to serve the Lord. But they have no real feelings for the people they lead. These people are not on the leaders' minds except during the hour or so they are together for their small group. The leader who does not have a heart for the people whom God entrusts him to lead is a leader who will never really succeed at the level or depth needed.

Paul was a great leader. Throughout his letters to the churches and to people, we read of his strong feelings for those whom he served. He longed for them, prayed for them, wanted to see them again. He was consumed with a passion for ministry, yes, but it was people who drove that passion.

In the same way, every small group needs a leader who is willing to give, not only of his time and talents, but of his heart and emotions. He needs to grow to love his people, to care intensely about their lives, to bleed when they bleed, to rejoice when they rejoice. And it all needs to be genuine. People know when it is not, and they are turned off. The true godly leader is so devoted to each member of his group that they almost become an extension of his own family. Such devotion goes a long way to make up for deficits in speaking ability and academic prowess. Especially in the '90s, people want to know how much you care. Then they will let you lead them.

There you have it. This is what it takes to have prepared leaders. They are leaders because they are called by the Lord and equipped by Him. They then dive in with all their heart and soul—committed to the Lord and to the group in order to help accomplish all the Lord has for the lives of each individual in their small group.

Eight Keys to Starting Small Groups in the Dynamic Church

Just as there are keys for preparing leaders, so we have found eight important keys to starting small groups in the Dynamic Church. Each key unlocks an essential part to having a successful, long-lasting small group ministry.

1. Evaluate Your Leadership Base and the Needs of the Church

The Leadership Base. We have found it helpful to keep a periodic update on all our leaders in order to utilize them to the maximum, yet not overtax any one person. The Dynamic Church will have many people who have leadership qualities, some deeply involved and others who still need mentoring to develop their full potential. Therefore we suggest you divide them into those who are currently in leadership and those who have been leaders but are not presently involved. In addition, evaluate their leadership capabilities: the top leaders you can consider to be "mentors"; those still needing training you can consider to be "disciples." Often your second string of leadership, whom we prefer to call "disciples," are at that level only because they lack training and opportunity to develop on-the-job skills.

Next, after deciding what small groups you wish to offer, determine who from your leadership pool can best assume the responsibility for the overall leadership of this ministry and who best qualifies to lead each group. You do not want to overload some of your current leaders, even though they may be the best qualified, as long as you have others who can do an acceptable job. What you may want to do is to choose two people for each position—one from the mentor group and one from the disciple group. The disciple can be mentored so he can eventually take over the group. In this way you can have your groups start out strongly and, when appropriate, have your lead mentor turn over the leadership to his disciple.

Needs of the Church. In chapter 8 we explained how to determine the needs of your church. Such an evaluation should be done periodically because needs can change as your membership increases. To remain a Dynamic Church, you need to stay abreast of the congregational needs and stay on the cutting edge.

2. Incorporate Prayer into Every Aspect of the Small Group

Prayer will be central to the success of all you do as a Dynamic Church, and it is no less so for the small groups. You will want to make prayer a central part of everything your group does. (Refer to chap. 8 on the Developing Church for the Seven Keys to Prayer.) Your small group leaders need to feel comfortable in their prayer skills, both in a group setting and privately. You should offer a small group on prayer periodically to help those who wish to improve their skills. We have found the topic of "drawing closer to the Lord" to be one that attracts many people.

Glen has coauthored a book, *Drawing Closer: A Step-by-Step Guide to Intimacy with God,*[2] which can be very helpful as a small group text or used alone. It is centered on prayer and our walk with the Lord. It is an excellent book to help people at any point in their Christian walk to discover which of six levels they are on in their walk with the Lord: knowing Him as Holy Sovereign, Savior, Father, Companion, Good Friend, or Intimate Friend. It gives you eighty-eight questions based on your faith and trust in the Lord in your daily life to help determine your level. The individuals then go to that level and work through the Action Steps of the level, which are all resourced in the back of the book. They work through each level until they complete the Intimate Friend level. The last chapter is called "What to Do in Dry Times." It identifies things that cause us to cool off in our relationship and shows us how to correct those problems.

Leaders need to pray regularly for their group also. Both the specific leader and the leadership of the church in general should have a strong sense of responsibility to pray for the various small group ministries the church has. These are your people, and God has given you the responsibility to care for them. *Pray for them* as part of that undertaking.

3 Empower the Vision

By the time your church has become a Dynamic Church you know the truth that "without a vision the people perish." In the past, your people have caught the vision for what God is calling you to. However, the trick is to keep that vision fresh, to keep it before the eyes of your people. We have found media to play an important part in this process.

The church needs to be reminded periodically that it has some sharp small groups. Word of mouth—hearing how lives have been touched and changed—is a powerful tool to increase vision for and the desire to be involved in small groups. This can be done through live testimonies of those who are involved both as leaders and as participants. It can also be done through video presentations if you have that capability. The same thing can be done through your church newsletter as people write about what their small group has meant to them.

When introducing a new series for a small group, an original skit can be used. Well-designed flyers and bulletin inserts, literature, along with periodic sign-up and information tables in places of high traffic are important in keeping the vision of small groups before the congregation. For the tables, it is good to have one or two personable, enthusiastic people who are there to answer questions, to enroll people, and in general to help the individuals catch the vision for what a small group can do for them.

You will also be wise to keep your leadership board of the church, such as deacons or elders, informed regularly of what God is doing through the small groups. This helps to keep before them the vision for small groups and lays the foundation for positive response when requests for finances, enlarging, or other needs are brought before them. It also helps prevent any corruption of the vision or misunderstandings from arising.

4. Express Your Commitment to Small Groups

For anything to succeed in the church, it usually takes strong, visible commitment by the pastor for the congregation to want to be involved. The pastor must regularly refer to small groups as possible application points or solutions to problems mentioned in his sermons.

As we have consulted with churches throughout the United States, we have repeatedly seen two common mistakes related to commitment:

Setting Your Goals Too Low. It is human nature to like the status quo, not to venture out from our safety zone. Therefore, churches can too often fall into the trap of limiting God by not establishing all the small groups He wants for the church. What is too little? This varies from church to church, but certainly the following would be pitfalls for all churches:

- Only one small group this year. The needs of the church are too varied to offer only one group. You need to have several groups in order to get the most people involved.
- Having only leadership be your small group. They need discipling, but you do not want them to be your only small group. You need to reach out and include as many others as possible.
- Goals that are too easy to reach. Goals that are in sight or are too simple are not fulfilling when you reach them. In fact, it can be a letdown to reach something for which you did not have to expend much effort. It is almost like making mud pies as an adult. What's the value even if you reach your goal of making ten thousand mud pies in a day?
- In the same vein, anything that you don't need to pray about you should not be wasting time on.
- If you can say at the end of the project, "I could have done this without God's help," you can be certain your goals were set too low.

The bottom line is: what is God asking you to do? Are you resisting or afraid? Why? Has He not promised over and over to guide us, to accomplish all His purposes for us if we let Him? (Prov. 3:5–7; Ps. 37:3–5; Isa. 30:21).

Trying to Reach Goals Too Fast. In our society, we try to do things quickly. This can happen in goal setting and when starting our small groups. There are two common traps of moving too fast:

- Starting before everyone has caught the vision. The leadership first must have the vision, and then it must be communicated to the congregation. Only when everyone is on board is it safe to move forward and start the groups.

- Starting before you have all your people in place. Sometimes we let our enthusiasm or the great need for a group push us into starting before we have everyone in place.

When we move too fast, we only create a weak foundation and set up future unnecessary problems—ones that might eventually bring down the program as disillusionment, discouragement, and lack of commitment set in.

5. Experiment with Different Types of Groups

God wants us to do His work with excellence. Jesus frequently said, "You of little faith." God wants us to trust Him, to reach out to try to be better than we currently are. These are signs of health, of growth.

But too often a church can get caught in the mistake of not keeping up with the current thinking and needs of society. God has placed your church in your community to reach the people He has living around the church. He wants and expects you to reach these people. So you have to be "all things to all people." This means you need to offer topics through your small groups that can attract people to attend. Some people might attend a small group though they would not attend a church service.

How about advertising a group on divorce recovery? Or one on addiction recovery, or one for single moms or single dads? Put it on your marquee; advertise in the local grocery stores and businesses; go door-to-door with flyers—do whatever it takes to contact people. This becomes not only a service to the community, but a wonderful way to evangelize. The Dynamic Church is one that is on the cutting edge of what God is doing. Experiment with different types of groups. After all, it is better to try and not succeed than not to try at all. And if the Lord is leading you to start a new group, know that He will make you succeed. Let it be written on your small group leader's tombstone, "At least he tried." And after all, isn't that what God wants us to do? To step out in faith for Him and to leave the results to Him as He accomplishes His purposes through us. But He cannot move through a stationary object. He needs our willingness to be on that cutting edge with Him, to risk failure. But know that even if you fail, you will learn lessons that God can use to strengthen your ministry. So go ahead—step out in faith, and God will catch you!

6. Expand Leadership Skills

A Dynamic Church is a living, growing organism that is constantly developing new needs as people grow in the Lord. New people come in, and in general, the Lord's blessings expand the borders of the church's calling. Due to this growth you will need to create new groups as God gives you leadership and (when needed) the host homes in which to do His work. It also means you will need to expand the skills of your leaders so they can take on these new areas. For example, as you see more and more divorced people attending, you will want to ask the Lord if you should start a divorce recovery group. You will want to know whom He wants to lead it, and in turn that person will want to pray about it. The individual will then want to study, pray, and plan what to present. He will want to search the available Christian literature for the right textbook(s). He will want to pursue resources like tapes, videos, literature, organizations, or other similar aids that can be helpful in the divorce recovery sessions. Even though he may or may not be divorced, he will want to start sharpening his skills and understanding by compiling information on questions and problems faced by divorced people and the different solutions or answers he feels are appropriate.

For those who are currently involved in small group leadership, you will want to offer at least quarterly times for training, for refreshment, and for evaluation so their skills are kept sharp. It is also helpful to gather different leaders together, to share what God is doing, and to talk about problems to see how others have dealt with similar situations.

7. Encourage Existing Groups

There is nothing like pastoral visits to a group to make it feel special, to encourage not only the leadership but the participants. We all grow up wanting our parents to recognize and applaud our efforts. The same principle holds true in the church. When the leadership recognizes what we are doing, it is special and even overwhelming, especially a large church. A pastoral visit is a simple way to encourage a group. It is very helpful to do this at the time of the group's start-up if you have the time and energy. We suggest that at least within the first month or so, where possible, the senior pastor should pay a short visit. It is better if he can stay for the entire meeting, but if he can't, it is OK. If he has just come from something and also has to run to another place, it impresses everyone that he cared enough about them to take time from his jammed schedule to drop in on them.

One of the ways we have found to encourage a small group aimed at newcomers is to have the pastor be the one leading it. For example, in the four series for new members where coauthor Glen Martin pastors, he leads the first one. Some churches are so large that many members have never talked with the pastor. Having the pastor lead the small group gives them contact with him from the first and provides a good bonding with him and with the church from the very start. It helps keep them in the church.

8. Energize Small Group Leaders

How? Make heroes of people. Just as we need to encourage many of the people who have served faithfully over the years, such as our children's leader who has been there for the last seven years enduring and persevering or the librarian who does her work well but gets little recognition, so we need to be aware that small group leaders can also get lost in the maze of all that is happening. When they first begin to serve, we usually are careful to encourage them and thank them. But as time goes on and things are running smoothly, it is human nature to take their service for granted because they are in leadership roles and are "doing their duty." When this happens, we are opening ourselves up for problems.

The Enemy of our church likes to get people focused on themselves. He likes to, as the Accuser of the Brethren, whisper in their ears, "You are unappreciated. Look at all you do every week. You spend hours in preparation, much time in praying for your members. When was the last time the pastor even acknowledged your sacrifice? He doesn't have to make a big deal of it. They are taking advantage of you and your good nature." Soon the person is thinking, *I don't need to be recognized all the time, but it would be nice to hear "Well done" or "I appreciate your hard work here at church." All I ever hear from people are complaints or problems. Maybe it is time to let someone else take this job. Then they will appreciate me!* Self-pity, getting our eyes focused on us and not the Lord, is an easy trap to fall into.

Why leave fertile ground for the Enemy to sow his weeds in? Take it away by planting your own seeds. They come in many forms, such as notes of appreciation once in a while or a word of encouragement when you see people in the hall or sanctuary or in a meeting. Mention your appreciation publicly, when appropriate, in meetings or even from the pulpit when you are featuring their ministry work. When you plant your seeds, the harvest will be a positive one in which it will be harder for Enemy weeds to take root. We suggest you visit key leaders in their homes or take them out for a meal. A small gift from the church or from yourself or a certificate of appreciation also serves to remind the person you care about them and are thankful to the Lord that they are an important part of what God is doing in your church. Certainly we see this principle in the writings of Paul who said, "I thank my God every time I remember you. In all my prayers for all of you, I always pray with joy because of your partnership in the gospel from the first day until now, being confident of this, that he who began a good work in you will carry it on to completion until the day of Christ Jesus. It is right for me to feel this way about all of you, since I have you in my heart" (Phil. 1:3–7a). What a great note of encouragement to those who enabled him to do God's work. How it must have lifted their spirits.

Dr. Paul Brand was speaking to a medical college in India on "Let your light so shine before men that they may behold your good works and glorify your Father." In front of the lectern was an oil lamp, with its cotton wick burning from the shallow dish of oil. As he preached, the lamp ran out of oil, the wick burned dry, and the smoke made him cough. He immediately used the opportunity:

"Some of us here are like this wick," he said. "We're trying to shine for the glory of God, but we stink. That's what happens when we use ourselves as the fuel of our witness rather than the Holy Spirit. Wicks can last indefinitely, burning brightly and without irritating smoke, if the fuel, the Holy Spirit, is in constant supply."[3]

Churches are a lot like this illustration: they will burn out easily if there is not a constant power source, the power of God at work in the church. One day we will all be called home, and there will probably be a tombstone placed upon the site where the remains of our bodies lie. People will walk by and say, "There lies old so-and-so," forgetting that to be absent from the body is to be present with the Lord. But on that tombstone there will be two dates. The first date will be the date of birth; the second date, the date of death. Date of birth . . . a dash . . . date of death. Friends, the date of your birth is of little consequence to most people. The date of your leaving will fade away as well. What really matters is what you do . . . with your dash. Did you impact the world for the kingdom . . . or not? Did people come to the Savior because of your influence . . . or not? The Dynamic Church accepts that responsibility and uses small groups as an integral part of the plan.

PART TWO

Two Effective Models

CHAPTER TEN

The Slow Track Model

Church leaders who have the vision for a small group ministry often want to start quickly. They want to use what we call the Fast Track Model for small group ministry, which will be presented in the next chapter. Most church leaders, however, do not anticipate the time and attention that founding and nurturing such a fast track ministry will require. Thus, many churches find that a Slow Track Model will work best for them.

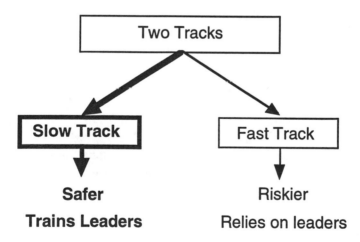

The Slow Track

The strength of the Slow Track Model is that it allows a church to move slowly. In addition to getting the process going through the establishment of a group, it also provides for the training of future group leaders. By training leaders, the expansion of the small group ministry is secured. The

Slow Track Model[1] is a solid way to begin a small group ministry in a local church that (1) is not quite ready for small groups, (2) has had a negative experience with small groups in the past, (3) doesn't have many trained leaders, (4) has an irrational fear of small groups, or (5) has never attempted a small group ministry before.

Start the Process with Education

Developing a new ministry begins with education. Someone must attend a workshop, read a book, or participate in a small group ministry. Then the vision of a small group ministry must be introduced to the church leaders and worshipers. It takes time to educate leaders and gain their support. In most cases it will take a minimum of one year to gain enough support to move forward.

Begin by preaching and teaching on biblical community. Be sure to develop your own support group of prayer partners who agree with your vision for the formation of a small group ministry in your church. At every opportunity share your vision for small groups in a general way with church leaders, boards, and committees. Use communication lines such as church newsletters, bulletins, programs, flyers, and one-on-one conversations. Communicate your vision for small groups in at least five different ways during the year.

Keep the training group visible to the congregation. Sometimes people who are not in the training group will be suspicious about what is happening in the group. Stress that this initial group is a "training" group and that eventually everyone who wants to be in a small group will have the opportunity. It is wise to have people sign up on a waiting list for the next training group or to join one of the new groups to be started.

Write a Vision Statement

Conduct a needs assessment of your congregation and the community beyond your front doors. Determine existing networks of people such as Sunday school teachers or people involved in youth sports. Wherever you find a group of people with similar interests, you have found a target group from which a small group may be developed. List all the possible networks of people and assess their openness to a small group. Determine the two or three most responsive groups and develop a vision for starting small groups for each target group.

Write a vision statement purposefully, precisely, and pictorially. Explain the purpose of your small group ministry (the biblical reason for it). Answer all the who, what, where, and how questions. And state exactly what such a ministry will look like once it is in place. Share this detailed vision and plan for a new small group ministry with the official board of your church to receive final approval (if needed).

Enlist a Core of Potential Leaders

Make a list of twenty to twenty-five people who might be receptive to being in a training group. Normally about half of those on your list will agree to participate. From your initial list, look for ten to twelve leaders who are interested and willing to explore the possibility of becoming leaders of future groups. There could be five to six couples or a mixture of couples and singles to equal ten to twelve participants. Mail them a letter telling them what you are seeking to do and why they have been selected to receive your invitation. Let them know you will be contacting them by phone or in person within two weeks to discuss the possibility of their involvement. Ten days to two weeks later, follow up with a phone call or appointment.

Once the membership in the group is determined, set a schedule for the meetings, including times, days, and location. If more than ten or twelve people agree to be in the initial group, consider starting two separate training groups that meet at different times or days of the week. This will take more of your time as the trainer but will deliver twice the leaders and groups later on.

Those in the group will learn to lead by experiencing group life themselves. The members of the group may be at different stages of their spiritual life and growth. Some may be deeply committed, others may be searching. They may be members of your church, another church, or regular attenders who have yet to make membership a priority. The group will provide each with an opportunity to be nurtured in both their congregational development and their individual Christian journeys.

Contract with Your Training Group

It is crucial to stress from the very beginning that this is a "training" group and that each couple or person is contracting (or covenanting) to lead his own group. Throughout the training period regularly remind group members of this fact. They easily fall into the trap of enjoying the group so much that they do not want to break up later on. If members have never experienced such an intimate fellowship before, they may go through a grieving process when the original training group disbands. While this response is not insurmountable, it should be recognized. Occasional get-togethers of all the group leaders enables those who are now leaders to stay in touch with those whom they first experienced the joys of small group fellowship.

Institute Training for Several Weeks

The group will meet together for a period of three to four months. Use the first meeting to get acquainted, to discuss the purpose of the group, and to introduce the curriculum. For the next two months the trainer should lead the group, allowing the group members to experience what a group is like and to see group leadership modeled. During the third month, allow the group members to take turns leading the group once each week. At the end of each of these meetings, debrief the practice session by offering suggestions as a group and one-on-one at a later time. This time of debriefing is called "process time."

Develop Individual Prospect Lists

At the beginning of the fourth month, begin to assist the group members to make prospect lists of people they would like to ask to be in their own small group. Lead them in times of prayer for their future groups and have them send out letters of invitation similar to what you did in recruiting them. Intentionally create new groups of only six to eight members so that there is room for new or prospective members to join.

Each training session begins with instruction on small group leadership. Following this training time, the group then moves into an actual small group session where the trainees experience what it's like to be in a group. At the end of the session, a short time is devoted to processing the experience. Notice that the training time goes down each week, but the actual small group experience remains constant (see figure 14).

Seek Out an Apprentice

Once the new groups are determined, have the group leaders recruit an apprentice who will assist them and be trained to begin another group. The term *apprentice* is important in that it communicates the idea that the person holding that title will advance to becoming a full-fledged leader. This is quite different from the term *assistant leader*, since that term communicates the idea that a person can be an assistant forever. The term *apprentice* helps build the idea of multiplication of groups.

Begin New Groups

Schedule the new groups to begin in the seventeenth week (the first week of the fifth month). This scheduling is vital to a healthy beginning. The last meeting of the training group should be in the sixteenth week. Plan on having a celebration of your time together and a dedication of the new groups. Members should then begin their own groups the very next week. The more time that elapses between the end of the training group and the beginning of their own groups, the greater the possibility becomes that the leaders will not lead their own groups.

Offer Continuing Education

At first the small group leader will need to keep tabs on the new group leaders by meeting with them on a regular basis. During the initial stages of the new group start-ups, it is best to meet weekly and then move to monthly meetings once the small groups are in place. The meetings should include discussion of resource needs and group problems, and the answering of questions. Encourage, resource, and support the new leaders in every necessary way until they gain confidence.

Repeat the Process

Once the new groups are in place, begin leading another training group. Go back to the first step in this chapter and begin the process all over.[2]

Figure 14

Weeks

| 1 | 2 | 3 | 4 | 5 | 6 | 7 | 8 | 9 | 10 | 11 | 12 | 13 | 14 | 15 | 16 | 17 |

Training Time Each Week

Actual Small Group Experience

Process Time Each Week

New Groups Begin

CHAPTER ELEVEN

The Fast Track Model

Some churches are naturally ready to start a small group ministry quickly. Such churches usually discover that they have a number of prepared leaders who may have received training in other churches or perhaps through a parachurch ministry.

The morale of the congregation is positive, and the worshipers have a vision of ministry to each other through small groups. There is no need to spend one or two years developing a vision for small groups among the people. They already have it. The congregation may be like a racehorse that senses the opportunity to run and cannot wait to get started.

If your congregation finds itself in the category of a Dynamic Church, then it is wise to move ahead quickly. Moving quickly, however, does not imply moving recklessly. You still need to organize, advertise, and train your people. You will simply be able to do it faster. Whereas in the Slow Track Model you might start five to ten small groups in one year, using the Fast Track Model you will most likely begin twenty or more.

Start the Process with Education

Even though your church may be excited and launch quickly into a small group ministry, it is wise to spend some time educating the leaders and congregation on your vision. It is especially crucial to educate members and groups throughout the church who may feel particularly threatened by the emerging small group ministry. If at all possible, try to involve all existing groups into small group ministry.

A solid process of education will include communication to your congregation through a minimum of five avenues.

1. Sermons. It is obvious that what is endorsed from the pulpit carries more status than what is never mentioned from the pulpit. This is why it is

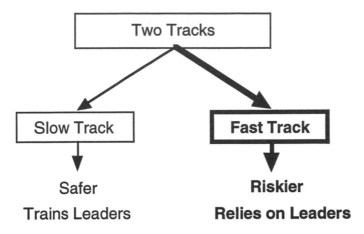

vitally important that the preaching pastor accepts and promotes the small group ministry. The congregation naturally looks to see what the senior pastor endorses. The senior pastor's role from the pulpit is to give the biblical rationale for the small group ministry and to provide an encompassing vision for the congregation. Details of exactly how the small group ministry will function can be provided at information meetings for those who are interested. However, the scriptural and emotional reasoning for the new ministry must be addressed publicly to the entire body.

2. Information Meetings. One or two informational meetings should be scheduled so that interested people can come to receive further details on the exact format of the small groups. At these meetings, individuals can ask questions and probe deeper into the workings and purpose of the small group ministry.

3. Personal Letters. A personal letter written to the congregation can be mailed to every member or family on the church's mailing list. The letter should come from the senior pastor or the director of the small group ministry. Through this means, all those in the constituency of the church can be informed of the new ministry. The letter may be two or three pages long and provide the basic purpose and vision behind the new ministry. Further details can be given on upcoming informational meetings plus phone numbers and people to contact for further information. Dates for leadership training and sign-ups for the small groups should be in the letter. If the letter is mailed before the pastor's messages on small groups, then the letter will include dates when the pastor will be introducing the new ministry to the congregation.

4. Group Meetings. In the weeks before the small group ministry kicks into full gear, a team of two or three leaders should make the rounds to all adult Sunday school classes, men's and women's groups, and as many existing small groups as possible to present the small group ministry and answer any questions. There is a normal fear among existing groups as to their future when the small group ministry begins. Effort should be made to enlist all existing groups to become a part of the new ministry. However, if some groups have been around for years, e.g., the women's missionary group, and they choose not to be involved in the new small group ministry, that is fine. Still, the more existing small groups you can enlist to be a part of the new ministry the better it will be.

5. General Communication. Be sure to advertise the new small group ministry in general church publications such as church newsletters, bulletins, and programs. The key is to communicate as much about the new ministry as possible through every available means. During breakfasts, lunches, and potlucks, be certain to mention the small group ministry and highlight its importance for the health and growth of your church.

Enlist and Train a Core of Leaders

What makes the Fast Track Model workable is the ready availability of small group leaders in the church. These leaders may have received experience and training from other churches or parachurch ministries. But you still need to provide a training time for them.

The leaders of your small group ministry should develop a training manual and workshop that can be taught in a six- to seven-hour workshop. The workshop can be held in an all-day Saturday format beginning at 9:00 A.M. and ending at 4:30 P.M. or on two evenings meeting from 7:00 P.M. to 10:00 P.M. Of course, whatever schedule works for your members is fine.

The training session should include the following seven key areas of training:

1. Purpose. State clearly the importance of small groups in the development of biblical community. Overview the different types of small groups that can be used and focus on the purpose, vision, and core values of small groups in your church.

2. Plan. Explain in detail your church's plan for small group ministry. Train the leaders in the essential elements you expect each group to use (prayer, Bible study, etc.), and review what the small group structure will look like. Be especially careful to outline how leaders will be identified, trained, and supported.

3. Pastor. The term *pastor* is used of all small group leaders to highlight their key role in pastoring those in their small groups. Thus this session will focus on the leader's role and responsibilities.

4. People. Use this session to stress the importance of teamwork and how to build cohesion among the group members. This is the time to point out how to recruit group members and select an apprentice and host.

5. Place. Discuss aspects of choosing a meeting time and place. Basic instruction on understanding room dynamics and how to create a "safe" environment and atmosphere are helpful.

6. Promotion. Note the ins and outs of how the small group ministry will be promoted and ways for the small group leaders to make their own group attractive to those they seek to recruit.

7. Process. Go over basic skills for small group leadership, such as how to ask questions and what to do if no one talks or if someone talks too much. Discuss problems to avoid and the basic reasons why small groups fail. Explain the life cycle of small groups.

The organization of your leadership training workshop may not follow the above ideas exactly, but the essential content should be included.

Advertise in Advance

Not only do you need to advertise for small group leaders, but you need to advertise for those who are interested in being part of a small group. Begin advertising at least two months before the first meeting of the small groups. Begin slowly and then increase the advertising as you get nearer to the starting date. One way to recruit possible small group members is to place a sign-up card in the church bulletin, program, and newsletter. (See sample on next page.) People can mail the card to the church office, hand it to an usher, or place it in the offering.

These cards can then be used to compile a list of interested people, which can be used by the small group leaders to recruit members to their groups. This list also serves as a way to predict how many small groups will be needed. In general it is good to have seven small groups for every one hundred people who are interested. Or, another way to figure it, you will need one small group for every eight to ten people who indicate an interest in being part of a small group.

**BETHANY CHURCH
SMALL GROUP
LEADERSHIP TRAINING**

Orientation Meetings:
Sunday, Aug. 21 or Aug. 28
5:00 P.M.

Training:
Tuesday, Sept. 6, 13, 20, 27
7:00 P.M.
or
Saturday, Sept. 17
9:00 A.M. to 3:00 P.M.

(All sessions will be held in room C of
the Educational Center)

Please fill out application tear off,
and place in offering bag

☐ YES! I / we will attend the Small Group
Leadership Training.

My / our areas of interest are:

☐ Leader ☐ Apprentice ☐ Host/Hostess

Name(s)_____

Phone _____

Have a "Sign-up Sunday"

One way to organize the new groups is for each leader to contact interested people and invite them to be a part of his group. The list of interested people compiled over a two-month period serves as a good resource for this approach. However, care should be taken to be sure that all those who indicated an interest are contacted.

Another way to recruit participants for small groups that creates higher energy and morale is to have a "Sign-up Sunday." Using this approach, the church schedules the Sunday worship service one week before the first small group meetings for signing people up for small groups. Depending on the available space, one way to accomplish this is as follows: The worship service focuses on small group ministry and then time is given as part of the worship service or immediately following for people to move into a fellowship hall, gymnasium, or onto a patio or grassy area to meet the small group leaders and to sign up for a group. The small group leaders should be seated behind tables or at booths built especially for this occasion. In addition, the leaders should have available a one-page overview of their small group. The information sheet should tell the time, place, and directions to the small group, as well as the purpose, content, and length of meetings. A sign-up sheet should be available at each table or booth with a limit of ten people being able to sign up for any group. Worshipers then freely can move around the various tables and booths, asking questions and signing up for the small group of their choice.

Begin New Groups

The key to the success of this approach is beginning the first small group meetings the *very next week* following the sign-up Sunday. The communication, advertising, training, and sign-up Sunday will create an enormous amount of excitement and anticipation for the small group ministry. Waiting several weeks or months to begin will cause this excitement to grow into despondency. The best way to launch the small group ministry is to explode off the anticipation by starting the very next week. Don't sign people up until you are ready to begin. This means it is wisest not to have a sign-up day just before summertime or Christmas or Easter. Careful planning here will help get the new ministry started effectively.

Seek Out Apprentices

The future growth of your small group ministry is determined by how successfully you develop new leaders. You can build leadership development into the small group ministry by using an apprentice system.

Some small group ministries use the term *coleader* or *assistant leader,* but this has a negative impact on the multiplication and growth of the ministry in the long run. The problem is associated with the implication that a person can be a coleader or assistant leader forever. In contrast, the term *apprentice* implies that a person will eventually move out of the apprentice role and into the role of a full-fledged leader. While some may think the terminology doesn't matter, if you are serious about multiplying small groups in the future, the term *apprentice* is the best one to use.

Two types of apprentices need to be identified and recruited: an apprentice leader and an apprentice host. The apprentice leader is included in all the leading activities and shares increased responsibility for shepherding the group members and leading the meetings over time. The success of the small group leader is seen in developing a new leader and multiplying another small group. The apprentice host works closely with the small group host to provide a comfortable setting for the meeting and to oversee any provision of refreshments.

Offer Continuing Education

Crucial for the ongoing multiplication of the small group ministry is continuing education of small group leaders, hosts, and apprentices. As the church decentralizes its ministry, it must centralize its training. Most churches have found that the best way to facilitate this ongoing training in our busy society is to require attendance of all leaders, hosts, and apprentices at a regular meeting. Some churches offer a monthly meeting, but many are discovering that the time pressures people are under makes a quarterly meeting more workable. How do you get the leaders to attend the training meetings? Put enough time into preparation for the meetings so that they *will want* to come. You don't push them; you pull them.

The ongoing training at Glen's church is called S. A. L. T., which stands for Shepherds Advanced Leadership Training. At each meeting, ninety minutes of time is given to vision building, skill training, and strategic planning. Since people tend to lose sight of the overall vision within two to four weeks, it is imperative that time be allocated in every training meeting to highlight the purpose, values, and vision for the small group ministry. One aspect of skill training should be taught, and time should be given for discussion and planning at each meeting. Many of the concepts in the chapters 12 through 16 can be used for leadership training and development.

PART THREE

Straight Talk on Small Groups

CHAPTER TWELVE

Discovering Leaders

Throughout the world entire nations and movements have changed as the result of strong leadership. One radical shift was the demise of communism. When Khrushchev pronounced his famous denunciation of Stalin, someone in the congress hall is reported to have said, "Where were you, Comrade Khrushchev, when all these innocent people were being slaughtered?"

Khrushchev paused, looked around the hall and said, "Will the man who said that kindly stand up!"

Tension mounted in the hall. No one moved. Then Khrushchev said, "Well, whoever you are, you have your answer now. I was in exactly the same position then as you are now."[1]

Any leader will be determined by what he flees from, what he follows after, what he fights for, and what he is faithful to. To look at these four statements is to realize that there is a void in leadership in America today. This void now has permeated the church and its mission to reach people for Christ, to assimilate them into the church, and to build them up in their faith. To turn this trend around, leaders must be willing to stand up and lead. But what does a leader look like? What are the characteristics of a leader who really makes a difference for God?

Seven Qualities of a Leader

Someone has said that everything rises and falls on leadership. This is especially true for a church wishing to start a small group ministry that will enable the church to generate deeper community. Probably the greatest picture of the need for leadership that is recorded in the Bible is seen in the Book of Nehemiah.

The Babylonians had sacked the city of Jerusalem and defeated the Jews. It appeared as if there was no possible way for the people of Israel to recover from this defeat. Time passed slowly, but the people held on to the glimmer of hope for their beloved city of Jerusalem.

The only problem with this vision was the need to rebuild the walls of Jerusalem, a seemingly impossible task. It was at this appointed time that God called Nehemiah to lead the people of Israel in performing this task. The rest is history, both for a people's faith and for a leader's vision. Nehemiah rallied, informed, motivated, and organized the people. They responded with earnest desire to get the job done and glorify God. Fifty-two days later, you might have walked around the camp and seen people washing off their trowels, putting away their hammers, and cleaning up. The job was finished—at last!

If you carefully read the first six chapters of Nehemiah again, you'll see that God has provided us with a curriculum we might call "The Basic Qualities of a Great Leader." These qualities are not only essential for the key leadership but also represent a basis for selecting and developing a group of future leaders who can maintain the energy and vision of a small group ministry.

1. A Leader Must Have a Passion for Ministry

Whatever the task may be, chairing a board, putting together a musical, or leading a small group, passion will determine, more than anything else, a leader's success. Look at Nehemiah's life. His passion caused him to lose sleep. He knew the walls were in disarray, and God's hand was upon him to accomplish this job. We hope that more than anything else in this book, you catch our passion for creating the kind of community in which unbelievers are drawn to our Savior and long for the closeness and acceptance they see in the church. We trust you catch our passion for leading God's people. Yes, you will experience the Law of the Whale: "When you rise to the top and blow, you will get harpooned." But leadership is not just an art and a calling; it's also an incredible privilege.

As you seek to establish a small group ministry, make passion a priority. People with passion can be trained to lead. Leaders without passion will not lead.

2. A Leader Must Have the Ability to Motivate Others

Without people, who needs a leader? Leaders inspire people to do their best. This concept is noted in the statement often heard at leadership seminars: If no one is following you, you are just going for a walk. A leader is only a leader when others follow. Nehemiah proved to be a leader after arriving in Jerusalem. He was able to educate the Israelites and motivate them to become part of the work in rebuilding the walls.

3. A Leader Must Have an Unwavering Faith in God's Power

Great leaders are people of prayer who long to tap into God's power—through prayer. They realize that nothing will be accomplished without God's hand upon it. Look at Nehemiah's life as a man of prayer. Before the walls were built, Nehemiah was on his knees. The first thing Nehemiah did when he heard about the walls of Jerusalem needing repair was to pray. Nehemiah 1:4: "When I heard these things, I sat down and wept. For some days I mourned and fasted and prayed before the God of heaven."

What's the first thing you do when you face a problem or get sick or get stressed out? You ought to pray. What was the first thing Nehemiah did when provided with the opportunity to approach the king about returning to Jerusalem? He prayed. Nehemiah 2:4–5a: "The king said to me, 'What is it you want?' Then I prayed to the God of heaven, and I answered the king." That's exciting! God had already moved the heart of the king. Wouldn't you have been excited? "Want . . . what do I want? I thought you'd never ask. I want to go to Jerusalem." The first thing he did was pray, and he received one of the greatest joys of all—to be in on an answered prayer. Right before Nehemiah's eyes, God answered Nehemiah's prayer. Do you know what that prayer probably was? I think Nehemiah prayed, "Lord, I can't believe it. It's time. Please don't let me blow it now."

What kind of commitment had Nehemiah made once he checked out how bad his city and country had become? To pray! Nehemiah 2:12b: "I had not told anyone *what my God had put in my heart* to do for Jerusalem. There were no mounts with me except the one I was riding on" (italics ours). Nehemiah was waiting to get God's direction. And as believers and leaders in God's church, the thing we need to determine, when the times are tough and the people aren't listening, is whose voice we will listen to as we seek to fulfill the impossible task of turning our cities and country around. Nehemiah was no ordinary man. Why? Because he was a man of prayer.

What about the times when Nehemiah was criticized? What did Nehemiah do? He prayed. Nehemiah didn't say a word to these critics. He never said, "OK you wing nuts, you asked for it." He fought his greatest battles on his knees. He bathed the opposition, the circumstances—everything—in prayer. He tells us to pray and keep going.

Nehemiah 4:6: "So we rebuilt the wall till all of it reached half its height, for the people worked with all their heart." Nothing was going to stop God's people from doing God's will. And if there was ever an age in which we need persistence in the church, it's today. We need people who will assume a task or a responsibility and stay with it until it's done.

Do you know what's interesting about the life and leadership of Nehemiah? Even enemies became best friends to fight God's work. Nehemiah 4:7: "But when Sanballat, Tobiah, the Arabs, the Ammonites and the men of Ashdod heard that the repairs to Jerusalem's walls had gone ahead and that the gaps were being closed, they were very angry."

When the work of God is being opposed, even natural enemies will come together and get unified real quick. That's how Satan works. So what did Nehemiah do? Nehemiah 4:9: "But we prayed to our God and posted a guard day and night to meet this threat." They prayed as if everything depended upon prayer, and they took action as if everything depended upon them. It's OK for you to pray for God to protect your house at night, but lock your doors. It's OK to pray, "Lord, please keep this car in good shape," but change the oil. There's a beautiful combination in the life of a believer when prayer and action come together. Nehemiah's journey was filled with prayers, and he constantly reminded the people of God's unwavering guidance, presence, and power. As you select leaders, look for people who are on their knees praying.

4. A Leader Must Have the Ability to Grow through Opposition

If you think you've got problems, take a look at the life of Nehemiah. He was constantly harassed from the first day the Israelites started mixing the mortar until the last hinge was mounted on the gates. Critics stay near and remain vocal anytime you seek to do something great for God. Nehemiah endured sarcasm, ridicule, threats, and lies. Yet he remained faithful to the task at hand, despite the opposition. He refused to get sidetracked by the people who didn't like his vision. He had the heart of a servant and the skin of a rhino.

What can be learned from opposition? Why did God allow this opposition in the first place? Leaders learn very quickly from adversity, and we believe a good leader will learn much.

A leader will learn that Satan wants to destroy his or her influence. Recent history has demonstrated the impact of immoral choices and unethical decisions on the life of leaders. Leadership debris is everywhere! This is especially true in the church. Why are leaders in the church so often criticized? We suggest four reasons: (1) Leaders confront sin. Anytime you place yourself in a position of responsibility for the lives of others and are willing to address issues in their lives, you will be attacked. (2) Leaders are change agents. Despite the informational age in which we live, people in general do not like change. Therefore leaders must take change seriously and plan carefully. (3) Leaders are safe targets. The theory is that a godly leader will not answer back. Leaders appear strong externally but may be torn apart internally by criticism and opposition. Nonetheless, most leaders are more preyed upon than prayed for. (4) Leaders face criticism because they give answers, especially when they are spiritual answers.

A leader will learn to stay on course and remain diligent. You might remember Nehemiah's plight in chapter 6. His enemies tried four separate tactics to stop the rebuilding of the walls of Jerusalem. Each time, Nehemiah was forced to learn quickly, discern their true intentions, and remain on course. The first attack came from Sanballat and Geshem, who sent messages to Nehemiah trying to get him to meet with them in the Plain of Ono. They intended to do Nehemiah harm. Nehemiah's response was to say, "Oh, no!" to Ono. He told these opposers that he was doing a great work and could not veer from the vision. The second attack came as Sanballat and his servant tried to frighten Nehemiah and his people from doing the work. He accused Nehemiah of wanting to rebel against the king of Babylon and set himself up as king. Once again Nehemiah responded directly and called the accusation a lie. Tobiah and Sanballat then launched a third attack by hiring a false prophet to try to get Nehemiah to go to the temple and shut the door. Nehemiah showed his wisdom by asking the prophet, "Why should I run? And who am I to go into the temple? I'd die!" The last attack came from the famous "hate mail" that is familiar to every leader. Nehemiah's came from Tobiah. But Nehemiah knew that any criticism that makes us less effective for God is not from God. Nehemiah stayed on track and remained diligent in listening only to the voice of the Lord. Thus, he did not succumb to enemy tactics.

A leader must learn to confront graciously. "Grace under pressure" was Ernest Hemingway's definition of courage. Every leader should have that statement etched across his wall. If you are a history lover, you no doubt have studied the life of Abraham Lincoln. No one has experienced more opposition, apart from our Lord Jesus Christ, in making a radical change than did Lincoln. Donald T. Phillips wrote, "In his four years as president, Lincoln endured all of the cruel antagonism and severe criticism directed at him. And the fact is, that he not only endured the slander but overcame it to secure victory in the Civil War and preserve the nation—a most amazing achievement. . . . On occasion Lincoln would stand up and defend himself to any and all detractors, especially if the false accusation was particularly damaging to the public's view of his principles."[2]

5. A Leader Must Maintain Balance in the Midst of Adversity

Any leader must maintain a balanced perspective on both the "sweet by-and-by" and the "dirty now-and-now." Nehemiah very early reminded the people what a mess the walls were in and that it was not going to be an easy job (Neh. 2:17). Yes, he challenged the people to remain diligent to their work, but he also positioned guards at strategic locations to protect the workers from attack. He was acutely aware of the negatives all around him while he remained positive about the responsibility that was given to the people.

Don't look for leaders who are so heavenly minded that they are of no earthly good.

6. A Leader Must Be a Servant Leader

All great leaders for God have a common characteristic—persistence. Paul reminds Christians for all eternity, "I press on"(Phil. 3:14). Near the end of his life, Paul declared, "I have fought the good fight, I have finished the race, I have kept the faith" (2 Tim. 4:7). The fifth chapter of Nehemiah demonstrates how Nehemiah accepted a promotion to be the new governor of the land of Judah (Neh. 5:17), and yet he was willing to sacrifice for the good of the people.

This kind of leader is not determined solely by natural abilities. J. Oswald Sanders illustrates this fact with a look at the life of St. Francis of Assisi.

On one occasion Brother Masseo, looking earnestly at Francis, began to say: "Why thee? Why thee?" He repeated it again and again as if to mock him.

"What are you saying?" cried Francis at last.

"I am saying that everybody follows thee, everyone desires to see thee, hear thee, obey thee, and yet for all that, thou are neither beautiful, nor learned, nor of noble family. Whence comes it that it should be thee whom the world desires to follow?"

When Francis heard those words, he was filled with joy, raised his eyes to heaven, and, after remaining a long time absorbed in contemplation, knelt praising and blessing God with extraordinary fervor. Then he turned to Brother Masseo. "Thou wishest to know? It is because the eyes of the Most High have willed it so. He continually watches the good and the wicked, and as His most holy eyes have not found among sinners any smaller man, nor any more insufficient and sinful, therefore He chose me to accomplish the marvelous work which God hath undertaken; He chose me because He could find none more worthless, and He wished to confound the nobility and grandeur, the strength, the beauty and the learning of this world."[3]

7. Leaders Must Not Only Start Well, They Must Finish Strong

Everywhere you look you'll see people rushing to get to the top, to be the hero, to set the standard. Somehow they think that being number one is the secret of fulfillment, so they must get there as soon as possible. We start well, but do we finish strong? This happens a lot with small group ministries. They are launched with great fervor and lots of excitement. But two to three years later, there are but a few small groups that remain and the majority of those that ended did not end well.

We are writing this book at a time in history when the Olympic Games are coming to Atlanta, Georgia. You cannot watch a sporting event on television right now without some promotion for another athlete who has dedicated his or her life to winning the gold. The sad part of watching the Olympics will be observing nineteen-year-old athletes who have already passed their "prime" in events they excelled in just two years ago. In some sports a twenty-five-year-old is put out to pasture. Unless someone explains that there is more to life than achievement or position, these kids are in for a depressing remainder of their lives.

In the entertainment field, nothing is more pathetic than a "has-been" actor or singer who is still trying to live off the one hit he had back in 1964. Can you remember the write-ups in the paper after "The Beatle Anthology"?

People either loved the two-day extravaganza or thought the Beatles should have just remained silent and enjoyed their retirement years. Aspiring celebrities push to get their picture on the cover of *Time* forgetting that once you've been on the cover—that's it! Next week our attention will be turned to someone else.

Only two things last forever—God's Word and people. No person, no business, and no ministry can maintain momentum indefinitely. So why not pace your leadership development to peak as you end it, rather than as soon as possible? Go out with a bang, not a whimper. Many people suffer from the so-called "Polaroid syndrome"—they are overexposed and underdeveloped.

When Moses told the people of Israel they would capture the Promised Land, he basically said this: "The LORD your God will drive out those nations before you, little by little. You will not be allowed to eliminate them all at once, or the wild animals will multiply around you" (Deut. 7:22). So pace yourself! Leadership is a marathon, not a fifty-yard sprint. The goal of a leader's life is not to finish first but to finish well.

What Is Expected and Required of a Care Group Shepherd?*

1. To be consistent and committed in living the Christian lifestyle with a daily commitment to prayer as a top priority.

2. To see the vision of Community Baptist Church and be loyal to its leadership, committed to accomplishing the great things that God has called us to do.

3. To be dependable and accountable to those placed in leadership over you.

4. To be led and controlled by the Holy Spirit.

5. To be a regular participator in a Care Group, either by leading a group or by assisting in the leadership of that group.

6. To be committed to attending the monthly S.A.L.T. meeting.

7. To wear the Care Group badge each Sunday. Be sensitive to the needs that people have and respond to their needs.

8. To meet someone new every week.

9. To work faithfully and diligently each week in doing the work God has called us to do.

10. To be a member of Community Baptist Church, complete the special Shepherd training, and be selected by the pastoral staff.

11. To be faithful in tithing and giving time.

12. To maintain a solid family life.

*Used by permission of Community Baptist Church, Manhattan Beach, California.

CHAPTER THIRTEEN

The Sour Seven

There was once a rich man who had a big dinner party for all of his friends at his home one night. When the dinner was over, he invited them all out into the back yard, where he showed them his Olympic-sized swimming pool in which was swimming a man-eating shark. He gathered all his friends together and said, "Now, for a little after-dinner sport, I'd like to challenge you here tonight that if anyone can swim from this side of the pool to the other side of the pool without being attacked or totally destroyed, I will give you either a million dollars, a ranch in the country, or the hand of my daughter in marriage."

Almost immediately he heard a splash and sure enough there was a guy flying through the water like you'd never seen before. He hit the other side and jumped out onto the decking. The shark didn't even know he'd been in the water. The rich man went over to the swimmer and said, "Sir, that's a swimming exhibition like I've never seen before in my life. I don't understand how you did it, but you won. First, would you like to have a million dollars?" "No, Sir." "Well, what about my ranch in the country?" The man said, "That doesn't interest me in the least." "What about the hand of my daughter in marriage?" "Uh-uh, I'm not ready to marry." "So, what do you want?" "I want the name of the fellow who pushed me in the pool—that's what I want!"

It is amazing how fast we learn when we're in a crisis situation. When the pressure's on and there's no turning back, we focus intently. What's true of life in general is true of leadership in particular. Wisdom is certainly learning from your own mistakes. But due to the rapid learning curve you find yourself upon right now, we propose that you learn from the mistakes of others as well. You do not have enough time to make all the mistakes yourself. The following are not necessarily mistakes as much as they are areas that have proven to inhibit and reduce the building up of community through a small group ministry. We offer the following "sour seven" as an opportunity for you to grow through the mistakes of others.

Sour 1: Poor Organization

Organization can make or break a lot of things, and small groups are no exceptions. Sometimes in a church context we find ourselves deciding to do something of value but then not putting in the kind of planning that we would in the business world. In the best of circumstances, we are going to run into some problems. But when we are too casual, we risk running into many additional problems that could be avoided. So we need to decide several key issues ahead of time.

Who will organize the small groups? This person will have the weight of the whole project on his shoulders. He needs to be a person who has vision, is organized, and can communicate his plans easily to others. It also helps if he is respected by the church members, since the small group program will be seen as a reflection of who he is.

Where does the buck stop? Does it stop with the head of your small group ministry or does it go further up the chain of command, even to the pastor? At some point you have to have a person who makes the final decisions on what will and will not happen.

We suggest that the staff person who oversees this ministry be the one who has the final say-so. However, he does have the right to delegate such decision making further down the chain of command, but he needs to be certain that whoever he chooses has the respect of those working under him.

How will materials be selected? Who determines what will be used? Is it a committee made up of church leaders, the small group itself, the staff leader, or the head of the small groups? The capabilities of your leadership will help determine what is best. Some people like to offer the group at least two or more suggestions and then take a vote. There is a danger in this, however, because when we strongly want something but are voted down, we can tend to get our feelings hurt and not embrace the chosen course with as much enthusiasm as we would have if we were told what we would study.

Who will resolve problems? This would seem self-evident to some, yet it is not always clearly defined when there are several in leadership who have a part in the small groups. Let's say you have a staff person who oversees the small group, but the one who is actually in charge of the groups is a well-respected leader within the church. In addition, there are several deacons or similar leaders who attend the various groups. When a problem comes up, who will solve it? Furthermore who is responsible for determining how the problems will be approached? It is very helpful and healthy for the church if such questions are addressed at the beginning so that no one can accuse you of taking sides or "stacking the decks" on any given problem.

Sour 2: Lack of Planning

Pastor Richards wanted to start a small group ministry in his church and did what many leaders in our country do: he started much too fast. He had three men identified as small group leaders. He then challenged the entire church to sign up for a small group. Little did he know that 104 would sign up. This required a minimum of 30 people for each group, thus defeating the purpose of small groups.

When we plan well, we save ourselves a lot of grief down the road. In fact, good planning includes looking down that road to see where the possible problems are and then designing your program to avoid or at least minimize such potential problems.

But we can just hear you saying, "Who can tell what's down the road?" Humanly speaking, that's true. This is why the Lord says we are to ask Him what to do and not lean on our own understanding (Prov. 3:5). He promises, "I will instruct you and teach you in the way you should go; I will counsel you and watch over you" (Ps. 32:8).

One of the ways the Lord instructs us is to lead us to those whom He has taught. Another is to learn from the successes and failures of others. Let us share with you some of the things God has taught others who began a small group ministry.

Start the new groups right after Easter and right after summer. Both of these times seem to be transitional times in people's lives when they feel most receptive to taking on a new project. These are without doubt the two best opportunities during the year.

Plan for the new groups to have a life cycle of nine to twenty-four months. Have you ever had a soft drink with so much carbonation that it almost goes up your nose as you drink it? It starts out highly charged, but as time goes on, it loses its fizz. Small groups are the same way. They can lose their fizz—their impact—if allowed to run too long or indefinitely. Therefore, as part of planning, it is necessary to understand the life cycle of small groups, which is usually one and one-half to two years (see chap. 16). Knowing this, you are wise to have them end before the cycle is over in order for the group not to lose interest in small groups. You want the group to stop while people are still enthusiastic, still finding help from their group. If you do, then when you start the new one after your break, there will be a greater return rate than if you had continued straight through and suffered the natural loss due to lack of interest or burnout. You also will maintain a higher reputation for small groups within the church.

To have the right context, it is important to understand the need for closure in order for people, especially couples, to commit to a small group. You need a clear beginning and ending date so that busy people can enter in, get something they need, and have closure. So what is the best time-frame? We suggest that nine months is the optimal life cycle for a small group. Some can start in fall and have them end in the spring. Others can start in spring and end before Christmas.

Plan ways to promote and advertise the small groups. We all recognize the need to advertise the start-up of a small group. But experience shows that you need to regularly advertise small groups in the church to attract new people to the church and to bring on board down the line present members who did not join a group when the small group ministry was organized.

Flyers used for advertising need to be eye-catching and sharp, showing what the theme of the small group is, for whom it is intended (men, women, singles, couples), how to sign up, where and when it meets, and other necessary information. If appropriate, be certain to mention if there will be child care. The availability of child care is often a key factor in some people's decision to be part of a small group.

We have found bulletin inserts to be the best way of advertising, with attention drawn to it during announcements. The flyer should be eye-catching and simple. Put it in three to four weeks ahead of time. Any earlier and people will forget about it or postpone their decision. We have found that giving a deadline for signing up helps. Obviously you can allow them to sign up later, but the deadline encourages people to decide and respond. Include in your insert a response mechanism with clear instructions as to where to leave the filled-out response.

Another good way to advertise is to have visible sign-ups in high traffic areas. This will allow people to meet someone involved in the groups who is excited about them. This connection will encourage new people to become involved.

The worship service offers two excellent ways to keep small group awareness in front of your congregation. First and foremost, the pastor should try to incorporate something on small groups as a part of the solutions to the problems that are raised by the sermon topic. Another excellent way of communicating the value of small groups is to have testimonies during the service of people who have been helped by their small group. These should be short but very specific. It is wise to help the people giving testimonies decide what they would like to say and maybe practice it a couple of times with someone before getting up in what may be an intimidating atmosphere of the service.

Identify leaders who have a vision and a passion for hosting the new groups. The small group atmosphere is important. Ideally, you will want to choose host families who enjoy having people in their home. Also consider the following questions when choosing locations for hosting small groups:

- Can the home easily accommodate the number of people expected?
- Does the location have sufficient lighting? If not, can the lighting be supplemented so that everyone will be able to read?
- Are there young children in the home who will constantly interrupt the group or make too much noise?
- Is parking adequate?
- Is the location easily accessible to those attending?

Admittedly, we do not always have the luxury of the ideal. Still this can be our aim. Certain things can be changed, such as bringing more lighting, having a baby-sitter for the children, or even getting couples who live close to each other to carpool if parking is a problem.

Sour 3: Geographic Emphasis

A guaranteed killer of most small groups is to make the mistake of grouping people according to their geographic area and disregarding their marital status, age, or interests. For the '90s this just doesn't seem to work well. What you may find is that people will try out a neighborhood group, attend for a while, and then many will drop out as they find they have too little in common with those attending. People today want to go to groups that typically represent their stage of life. They want fellowship, identification, and the freedom to discuss their problems without being judged.

They want to know that fellow group members will be able to identify with where they are in their walk with the Lord, understand their struggles, and not be spiritual giants who have already slain most of the "Goliaths" in the world. They want to hear how someone just like them has faced this problem and had victory in it with the Lord's help. They don't want to be intimidated by the older people who too often jump in with the answers to the discussion questions, leaving them behind or intimidated. There has to be a pull, a satisfaction, a felt need being met by the group. Such things are accomplished better by designing the group to minister to a specific kind of people.

One church Glen consulted with in the early '90s determined that the people were going to be encouraged to attend a small group meeting within walking distance of their homes or at least a minimal drive. Upon looking at a map, Glen determined that one part of the church's area of influence had been grossly neglected because a certain age segment of the church was not ready to go to small group meetings. Several groups in the church had a vision for cross-generational fellowship but had been inhibited from pursuing this ministry because of the geographical mandate. This ministry was headed for either an explosion, with people becoming angry at the leadership's tunnel vision, or an implosion, with people becoming closed to the idea of the body being one. Geographically determining where people must attend is a sure way of creating stress and limiting the impact of the overall ministry.

Sour 4: No Leadership Development

Once you have good leaders in place, it is important to start training another generation of leadership. (Where appropriate, you can even do some of this while training the first generation of group leaders.)

As with the first group, they will need to be prayerfully identified so you can groom them and dispatch them into the ministry. This second generation is very important for several reasons. They will serve as backups if a leader is sick, is called out of town, goes on vacation, or is suddenly transferred. You or someone else may have to step in for a short period, but at least you will have a person who is partially trained to take over in the near future.

If your small group is successful, and it should be, it may grow to the point that you will need to form another group. Or, as is typical, you will identify another type of small group that needs to be offered, such as a recovery group, a divorced group, older singles, single parents, or some other more specialized group. You will need trained leaders to take over these new groups. By having trained the new leaders before they are needed, you will have had an opportunity to evaluate their effectiveness and have a sense for their ability to tackle the new groups. This will give you more confidence and less of a sense of playing catch-up when the unexpected happens or when your group is growing faster than you had planned.

The wise small group leader is always training new leaders so that the church can have as many people as God desires, and who are willing to be trained. This gives you a wonderful, broad leadership base from which the whole church can draw and benefit.

Sour 5: Forced or Set Curriculum

In years past, it was popular to have everyone studying the same thing in all small groups, partly to have unity and to cut down on the preparation times for those handling more than one group. In the '40s, '50s, and even '60s, this seemed to be acceptable. But it definitely is not a model for the '90s. As we have already alluded to, couples want to study young couples' problems, seniors are no longer interested in rehashing child-rearing problems although they can give insights, and the single person is put off by people talking about problems with their children. Only offering one curriculum is a sure way of limiting the number of people who will come, of dampening enthusiasm, and, in general, of making what should be an exciting, stimulating, and beneficial time just a routine church meeting that is attended more out of obligation than desire.

Sour 6: Bad Timing

In Ecclesiastes 3 we are told that there is a right time for everything. In the same way there is a wrong time for good things. We have identified three categories of wrong times for good things when considering small group ministry.

1. For the church. There are two wrong times in the church: (1) right after a split, when feelings are sensitive and raw and things need to settle down into the new routine; and (2) after there has been a power struggle in the church. Small groups need a nurturing atmosphere in which to thrive, and these times are less than ideal for planting a new small group.

2. For the leadership. Leadership needs to catch the vision before starting. Vision is a unifying factor. If the leaders in your church lack your vision for small groups and you start anyway, you are asking for problems. In fact, the Scriptures tell us that we can perish without a vision. Anything that is to work smoothly must have the full backing of those who are in leadership, especially when we are talking of spiritual matters. The Enemy of our souls does enough to stir up troubles without giving him an invitation through lack of unity or commitment to the vision of where God is leading. People who lack vision also do not know where they fit in, so they can feel as if they are on the outside or like a fifth wheel. This is dangerous because these people can undermine a leader to the point that he may no longer want to be in a position of leadership, or he may not give the backing to the project that is needed.

3. For the staff. The members of your staff are key to all that is done in your church. They need to be ready to help in the training of leaders. If they are not, you will be wise to hold off on starting your small groups. You may find they lack the vision to see why small group leaders need to be trained or they can't see that the time they invest in training now will be multiplied back to them many times over once they have trained leadership. Help them to see how these new leaders can shoulder some of the burden or workload they have had to bear alone until now.

The staff members may be unaware of how small groups will help further their own goals by enhancing the ministry for which they have responsibility. You will want to help them catch this vision. You may also need to help them analyze their own schedules to see how to incorporate leadership training into their activities as a priority.

For those staff members who do not know how to train another, you may want to help by giving them ideas or referring them to some good books on the subject. Encourage and show them that you have faith in their ability to train others.

Another potential problem arises when staff members do not know how to delegate. They are such go-getters, so creative and productive, that they may always want to be the ones in control or may never have learned the skills necessary to delegate. You will need to train such people in delegation and supervision.

Sour 7: The Wrong Context

Because you want your small groups to meet the needs of the broadest range of your congregation and you want to have the best context for meeting, we strongly suggest that, if at all possible, you target three major groups. When they meet you will want to convey the context for that particular group.

The first of the three groups consists of men, only so the men have the freedom to discuss in a manly way the things that are meaningful and perplexing to them. Since this often deals with the opposite sex, they need the freedom to discuss such problems among themselves without the inhibition of women present. Most men will not share their gut-level feelings in the presence of women.

A second grouping would be for women only. They, too, have their unique way of approaching subjects and need the freedom to express their opinions in a way other women will appreciate. It is also important to note that with the abuse many women today have experienced, the most needy women in your mixed groups will not openly participate at a level that will truly meet their needs. They will either not attend or stay on the sidelines, often for a subconscious reason. Unless they are looking for female companionship, single men will often be turned off by the discussions generated by women in a mixed group setting.

Couples and mixed singles groups, the third grouping, seem to be the only place to successfully have mixed groups.

Let's explore this a little deeper. Each small group is unique to itself. But there are some dynamics that need to be understood so as not to violate the context of the make-up of a group. Therefore, it is important to know the differences between how men think and feel versus how women think and feel. If you treat a women's group the way you treated your men's group, or vice versa, you are looking for a smashed nose as you fall flat on your face.

Take intimacy as an example. Men see intimacy as a threat while women value it as part of their security. If you talk to a men's group about intimacy in their walk with the Lord in the same way you would with only women, you will find problems and lack of connection with the men. Just because the session on intimacy with the women was a big hit, does not automatically mean it will be with the men. Men will most likely need a different approach if they are to embrace this concept.

However, in other areas, when you add the factor of a mixed group, you double your need for skill in handling a topic that needs different approaches or perspectives in order to be communicated to your listeners. A good example of this is that men are problem solvers and like to ask a lot of questions and hear the bottom line up front. On the other hand, women communicate through dialogue and like to go through the steps of the processes before reaching the bottom line. This difference in approach can be a formula for disaster if the leader does not know how to satisfy both types of needs in a mixed group.

So how do you keep from souring? By keeping focused on your goal. You have to know the Lord has called you to the task—in this case, to develop small groups. If you don't know this, then you will surely miss your target when difficulties come, and you'll find that the resulting confusion will sour the situation.

Clarence Jordan knew this truth. He was a man of unusual abilities and commitment. He had two Ph.D.'s, one in agriculture and one in Greek and Hebrew. So gifted was he that he could have chosen to do anything he wanted. He chose to serve the poor. In the 1940s he founded a farm in Americus, Georgia, and called it Koinonia Farm. It was a community for poor whites and poor blacks. As you might guess, such an idea did not go over well in the Deep South of the '40s.

Ironically, much of the resistance came from good church people who followed the laws of segregation as much as other folk in town. The townspeople tried everything to stop Clarence. They boycotted him and slashed workers' tires when they came to town. Over and over for fourteen years they tried to stop him.

Finally, in 1954, the Ku Klux Klan had enough of Clarence Jordan, so they decided to get rid of him once and for all. They came one night with guns and torches and set fire to every building on Koinonia Farm except Clarence's home, which they riddled with bullets. And they chased off all the families except one black family who refused to leave.

Clarence recognized the voices of many of the Klansmen, and, as you might guess, some of them were church people. Another was the local newspaper's reporter. The next day the reporter came out to see what remained of the farm. The rubble still smoldered and the land was scorched, but he found Clarence in the field, hoeing and planting.

"I heard the awful news," he called to Clarence, "and I came out to do a story on the tragedy of your farm closing."

Clarence just kept on hoeing and planting. The reporter kept prodding and poking, trying to get a rise out of this quietly determined man, who seemed to be planting instead of packing his bags. So, finally, the reporter said with a haughty voice, "Well, Dr. Jordan, you got two of them Ph.D.'s, and you've put fourteen years into this farm, and there's nothing left of it at all. Just how successful do you think you've been?"

Clarence stopped hoeing, turned toward the reporter with his penetrating blue eyes, and said quietly but firmly, *"About as successful as the cross. Sir, I don't think you understand us. What we are about is not success but faithfulness. We're staying. Good day."* Beginning that day, Clarence and his companions rebuilt Koinonia, and the farm is going strong today.

When you believe in something, you have a compelling drive to finish what you start. If you genuinely believe that small groups are essential for creating community among the members in the church, then, like Clarence, you will be driven to faithfulness as well.

CHAPTER FOURTEEN

Organizing for Growth

A local church is healthiest when it is growing. Just as it is natural for our bodies to grow and develop, so also a church's small group ministry is healthiest when new groups are released and new people are involved. Organizing for a healthy small group ministry requires two elements: organization of the larger ministry and multiplication of individual small groups.

The Jethro Organization

The "Jethro Principle" found in Exodus 18:17–27 provides the outline for organizing the overall small group ministry. Jethro's advice to Moses suggests four levels of leaders: 1,000s, 100s, 50s, and 10s, and three levels of organization. The leaders of 10s, of course, correspond to the leaders of each small group. Based on the Jethro Principle, it appears that God gifts enough individuals in a church to lead every ten people. To illustrate, a church with 150 adults might expect to have at least fifteen people who are capable of leadership at the level of 10s, that is, able to lead ten others. The church should have three people who are leaders of 50s and at least one person who is a leader of 100s. A church of 1,500 could expect to have 150 leaders of 10s, 30 leaders of 50s, 15 leaders of 50s, and 1 leader of 1,000s.

Level One. As soon as a small group ministry has five small groups it becomes a Level One Organization, as pictured in the following figure.

Level One Organization

This initial organization incorporates five leaders of 10s, each leading one small group. Five small groups of 10s equals a total of fifty people, which then requires a leader of 50s.

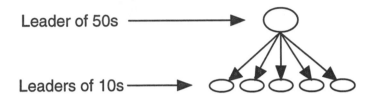

Level Two. As new small groups are multiplied, the stress on the leader of 50s increases. If this leadership structure does not expand, the overall small group ministry will stagnate because the leader of 50s will not be able to oversee, train, and resource many more groups. To grow, the ministry must move into the next level, which is Level Two Organization.

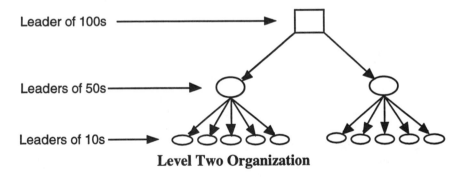

Level Two Organization

The need for Level Two Organization becomes apparent when there is a minimum of ten small groups, since it calls for a leader of 100s to step forward (10 X 10 = 100). This level potentially can exist until there are twenty leaders of 50s, who each oversee five leaders of five small groups each. Twenty leaders of 50s call for a leader of 1,000s (20 X 50 = 1,000).

Level Three. At some point in the continued expansion of Level Two Organization, the main small group leader must become a paid staff member, as the responsibilities become too much for a part-time volunteer. And, in the majority of situations, this takes place when the small group ministry grows beyond twenty small groups and almost always by the time there are fifty small groups.

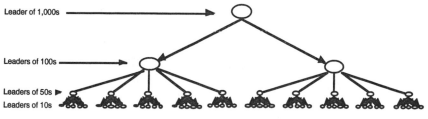

Level Three Organization

Very few churches get to Level Three Organization but those that do almost always have a full-time paid staff person who oversees the ministry.

It is entirely possible that you will not follow the exact organizational development as presented in the Jethro Principle. In designing your structure, you will need to weigh all the factors of your precise situation. Yet, the basic fact remains that you must continue to expand your organization. The lack of expansion will cause the entire small group ministry to stagnate simply due to the large span of oversight that will be demanded of the overall small group leader.

Multiply Small Groups

Active membership in your groups will not grow indefinitely. Your groups will reach a saturation point. While groups may briefly grow above the saturation point, they will soon drop to or below it. New members may join, but others will drop out. Figure 15 illustrates how a group grows above and then drops below its saturation point on a regular basis.

Figure 15

The saturation level is determined primarily by size. Small groups tend to saturate at fifteen people, adult Sunday school classes at thirty-five, and lecture-oriented classes at ninety to one hundred. Longevity also is a factor in saturation, as all types of groups seldom grow after two years.

Whenever a congregation reaches a worship attendance of two hundred, it is impossible for individuals to relate as a family. Therefore, as a church gets larger, if the needs for fellowship and intimacy are to be met, the congregation must be broken down into smaller units. A study conducted several years ago found that the average church member only knows sixty people by first name. As a church gets larger, people tend to know a smaller percentage of the people by first name, which can cause them to feel lonely and out of touch.

A principle of church growth is: to get larger you have to get smaller. This means that as a church gets larger it must get smaller by the development of small groups. To determine how well your church's small group ministry is doing, complete the following evaluation.

Total Number of Small Groups. As a rule of thumb, a church needs seven small groups for every one hundred adults present at its Sunday morning worship services.

For example, a church averaging 150 adults at Sunday morning worship services needs ten small groups (150 ÷ by 100 = 1.5 X 7 = 10.5).

Complete the following:

1. Your average weekly adult worship attendance is _____.

2. Line 1 divided by 100 equals _____.

3. Line 2 multiplied by 7 equals _____ small groups needed.

4. Total small groups available in your church is _____.

5. Line 3 minus line 4 equals _____ more small groups needed.

New Small Groups. A church may find that it has enough small groups based on the 7:100 ratio noted above. However, this is not the total picture. Since established small groups tend to resist the inclusion of newer people, it is important to have newer groups available that are open to the addition of new people.

As a general rule of thumb, a small group will close to the addition of new people between the eighteenth and twenty-fourth month of its existence. Thus, a church could have enough small groups, but if they are all over one-and-one-half-years old, the church would still have a problem.

In general 40 percent of a church's small groups should be less than two years old.

Complete the following:

1. How many small groups does your church currently have? _____

2. How many groups are less than two years old? _____

3. Line 2 divided by line 1 equals _____ percent less than two years old.

Total Number of Participants. Even with the best small group ministry available, not all of your adults will choose to participate. Generally speaking, a healthy church will have 50 percent of its adult worshipers participating in its small group ministry.

Complete the following:

1. Our average weekly adult worship attendance is _____.

2. The average adult attendance in our small groups is _____.

3. Line 2 divided by line 1 equals _____ percent of adults in small groups.

Using the above calculations will give you a rough idea of the number of small groups you have and the number you will need to begin. A small group ministry is healthiest when new groups are constantly being birthed. We all recognize that our natural bodies stay healthy because of cell division. The cells in our bodies regularly split and divide to keep us physically fit. The same principle applies to small groups in the church.

Asking a small group to split and divide is often met with resistance. The terms *split* and *divide* are not happy words to most churches. They conjure up memories of negative attitudes and mean-spirited people leaving churches. Yes, a church split is a painful event in which relationships are broken, such as in a divorce. It is for this reason that we strongly recommend that you not use terms such as these. In their place use words like *releasing, multiplication,* and *birthing.* God clearly wants us to release people for ministry, multiply His body, and birth new groups. These words are life-giving as opposed to life-sapping.

Pastor Ric Lehman of Ft. Collins, Colorado, wrote:

> Small groups can potentially turn God's people into an army rather than an audience. For this to happen though, a major lie of the enemy must be exposed: "When small groups divide, relationships are severed."
>
> Contrary to the life of severed relationships, small group multiplication is a unifying force in our fellowship. If there is a continual growth and birthing process, you will find a networking of relationships taking place, and community is developed in a larger fellowship. On the other hand, if a fellowship has small groups without releasing leaders from the existing groups, you end up with cliques and closed doors.[1]

To understand how multiplying groups actually increases the community of God's people, one only has to look at the twelve disciples. Is there any doubt that Jesus expected the Twelve to multiply? Could the fellowship and community of faith that is described so well in Acts 2:42–47 have taken place if the apostles had selfishly remained in their own small group? The answer is obvious, isn't it? The strategy of Jesus Christ was to reach the world through multiplication. In John 15, He clearly points out that bearing fruit—reproducing—is the purpose of the vine and the branches. Small groups only bear this kind of fruit when they unselfishly release leaders and members to begin new groups.

Five Ways to Release Energy

How then are groups multiplied and leaders released?

1. Keep sharing the vision for multiplication. From the very beginning of your small group ministry, make it part of your philosophy to release new leaders and begin new groups. Pastor Rick Lehman shares how this was accomplished in his church:

Our pastoral team has always believed small groups need to focus beyond themselves, yet we were seeing no fruit of that belief.

In analyzing our situation, we realized that our statements—both written and verbal—had not communicated our true intentions.

We were using words like nurture, relationship, family, kinship, fellowship. We did not talk, in the small group context, of outreach, evangelism, training, equipping, army. Without realizing it we were enabling a "take care of me" attitude in our groups—"inreach" without outreach.

We reworked our small group philosophy to include outreach, using statements like:

"One of the major avenues for reaching our city is through small groups."

"Imagine our city saturated with hundreds of small groups."

"Relationships and nurture cannot be separated from the mission of the local church."

"The small group is the launching place for all ministry involvement."[2]

2. Train new leaders. Each new group needs a leader, thus it is vital to an ongoing small group ministry to develop leaders. The most effective way to accomplish this is to institute an apprentice or intern system. The terms *apprentice* or *intern* build an expectation that they will eventually lead their own group.

3. Remain focused outward rather than inward. Except for special support groups and covenant groups designed for intimate sharing and caring, small groups that don't multiply are not following Christ's model of a small group.

4. Stop groups from saturating. All types of groups tend to saturate within eighteen to twenty-four months. The group must multiply within nine to eighteen months or it may never happen. If the group resists multiplying before the end of two years, it will most likely never do so.

5. Choose the right way to multiply. Karen Hurston, a specialist in small groups and author of the *World's Largest Church,* suggests the following three ways to multiply small groups.

Three Ways to Multiply Groups

An analysis of the various ways to multiply groups results in three basic approaches.

1. The Cell Concept. Cells in the human body often divide by splitting in half. Each half then becomes a separate cell. Small groups can follow this pattern with the leader taking half of the people and the apprentice taking the other half. Both establish their own small groups, select another apprentice leader, and begin to grow.

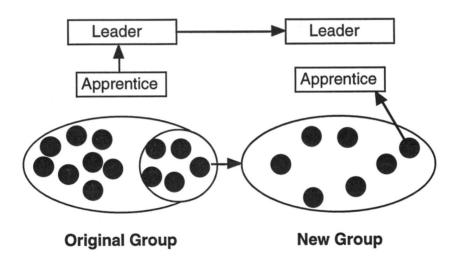

Original Group   **New Group**

2. The Missionary Group Plant. The small group follows the pattern of sending out (a missionary being one who is sent) its apprentice to begin a new group. The apprentice takes one other person from the original group who becomes his apprentice. Other than that one person, no other people are drawn from the original small group. The new missionary group plants its own small group by inviting others to join them.

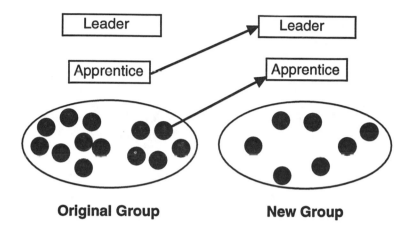

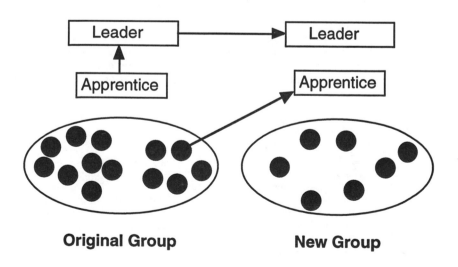

3. The Group Planter Method. Using this approach, the leader of the original group leaves to start a new group. He takes only one additional person from the group, who becomes his apprentice in the new group. The original apprentice then becomes the new leader of the original group. This approach works well because the apprentice continues on with a group he already knows.

How to Multiply Your Small Group

A. When are you ready to multiply?
  1. When the group is averaging fifteen or more people in attendance each week.
  2. When your apprentice has completed "Small Group Shepherds Training."
  3. When your Small Groups Pastor has given his approval.
B. How to prepare your group to multiply
  1. The Small Group Shepherd initiates a meeting with the apprentice to discuss the multiplication process. They pray, discuss, and agree together on the following:
      a. Who will stay in the current situation, and who will leave to begin a new small group? (The best scenario is for the apprentice to stay and take over the current group and the Small Group Shepherd to leave with approximately four to six people.)
      b. The one who is leaving decides which four to six people in the group he wants to challenge to go with him. One of the people should be a potential host or hostess for their new Small Group.
         The Small Group Shepherd and apprentice need to be in complete agreement on the above people. (If there is any problem, the "edge" should always be given to the apprentice.)
  2. At the next small group meeting, the Small Group Shepherd should begin to prepare the group members for the upcoming multiplication. Share with them the following:
      a. "As you know, our group has been growing, and we're looking forward to multiplying in order to reach out and minister to more people with Christ's love. Would you help us out by praying and allowing God to prepare your heart for this change? The apprentice and I have met, talked it through, and feel that God is giving us the green light on reproducing our group."
      b. Share with them who will be leaving (the Small Group Shepherd or the apprentice) and the approximate date when this will happen (about a month down the road).
      c. Share with them that no one will be forced to "go" or "stay." It is their choice. A few people might be approached on an individual basis to "go" with the ones leaving.
      d. Ask if they have any questions.
  3. The one who will be leaving now should talk individually to the potential host/hostess couple, asking them to consider becoming the host/hostess for the new small group. Ask them to let you know their decision by the next week.
  4. The one who will be leaving should talk individually with the other four to six people he has in mind, asking them to consider going with them to start the new small group. Ask them to let you know their decision by the next week.
         IMPORTANT: The Small Group Shepherd and the apprentice should agree upon every person who is asked to "go" or "stay" before he/she is approached.
  5. The Small Group Shepherd and apprentice should meet again to discuss the results of their discussions with members of the group and to agree on two dates:
      a. The final date of the original small group. It might be nice to have a potluck, an affirmation time, and prayer and commissioning for the ones leaving.
      b. The starting date of the new small group. They should also know the place, day of the week, time, and material they will use.
  6. The Small Group Shepherd shares with the small group what has transpired, who will be leaving, and the above dates.

CHAPTER FIFTEEN

Developing Leaders

A young couple attended church regularly to listen to a very wise pastor preach. Late one afternoon, they happened to find the pastor alone and thought this would be a great time to ask him a question that was weighing heavily upon their hearts. They shared with the pastor about several times in their lives when they were filled with doubts and fears. They had heard the good news of salvation and believed in it, but there were many times when they felt that they had not really been changed by it.

The wise pastor smiled, signifying his understanding of their personal struggles. He then went on to address their doubts in an unusual manner by asking them, "Where do you live?" The young man replied, "We live in Dayton." "Yes, of course," the pastor continued, "But your accent suggests you have lived somewhere else." The young man quickly responded, "Yes, I was born and raised in Kentucky." The pastor followed by inquiring about relatives who still lived in Kentucky. The woman proceeded to explain to the pastor that they visited their family and friends several times a year. "Having traveled and returned so many times from here to Kentucky," the pastor continued, "certainly you must know the way very well by now."

The two nodded in agreement. "I might say that I could almost drive to Lexington blindfolded," the young man answered, "I've made the trip so many times." The pastor then asked if their friends in Dayton knew they were originally from Kentucky. "They must know that you know the way from here to there," he suggested. "Of course," the woman replied, as if it were obvious.

"Suppose," the pastor asked them, "one of your friends asked for directions to Kentucky. Would you hide anything or would you explain the trip to them clearly?" The young couple responded that they always tried to give the best directions they could. "Can you guarantee that those people will be able to reach this destination?" the pastor asked. The couple responded, "Only those who follow the directions carefully."

There is a definite need for finding the next generation of leaders who will "follow directions carefully." In light of this fact, there is also a great need for leaders who have already been there and can train them in which way to go. The '90s has issued in a new paradigm for leadership. There has been a movement toward team leadership and team ministry. To illustrate these changes, we have put together the following chart that identifies the primary shifts seen in today's churches.

Leadership Paradigms[1]

Old Paradigm	New Paradigm
1. Only the pastors provide care	1. Both pastors and members provide care
2. Pastors alone equip the people	2. Training is done by gifted and trained people in the church
3. Certain spiritual gifts are only for the clergy	3. All Christians have the potential to receive the gifts
4. The pastor is a "player"	4. The pastor is a "player-coach"
5. Recruitment is based on the needs of the church	5. Quality ministry covers all the bases
6. Institutional recruitment	6. Relational recruitment
7. People serve out of a sense of duty; it is rarely enjoyable	7. People find church work very enjoyable and rewarding
8. Ministry has a competitive atmosphere because ministers are not called	8. Ministers give it their best because they are called by God
9. Ministers serve because of guilt	9. Ministers serve because of the blessing and challenge to grow
10. Competition in ministry	10. Team players in ministry
11. "Pastor's little helpers"	11. Fellow pastors
12. The pastor is the top	12. The pastor is "first among equals"
13. Little biblical basis is given for people's involvement	13. The Bible becomes the ministry manual for all God's people
14. Ministries last as long as the dynamic leader is still around	14. Ministries last indefinitely and grow as the leadership is shared and passed on

Skills for Leaders

Lao-tzu (604–531 B.C.) said, "A leader is best when people barely know he exists. Not so good when people obey and acclaim him. Worse when they despise him. But of a good leader who talks little when his work is done, his aim fulfilled, they will say, 'We did it ourselves.'"

In a general way, leaders need to express their personalities and styles of leadership by being real enough to open up their lives to let people know that they hurt, hope, and feel in the same way the people do. Don't play it safe. Any meaningful relationship requires a high degree of vulnerability. There is risk in loving: the risk of being laughed at, misunderstood, and rejected. To love deeply means that there will be hurt and conflict.

- Identify with people. Be yourself, the special person God created you to be. Don't try to be "spiritual." Keep the study on a practical level. Share common interests beyond the spiritual realm.
- Listen to people. Who are the people who have helped you the most in a crucial situation? It was probably not the advice-givers. When we give advice, we put ourselves in a superior situation. To press for change, however subtly, indicates that the person is unacceptable as he is.
- Affirm people. Jesus had a very different style. He believed in people, affirmed them, called fisherman to be apostles, loved prostitutes, Pharisees, and Samaritans. People found hope because of their relationship to Jesus. Look for the strengths and realize that each group is likely to have one or more unusual "characters" who need acceptance too.
- Love specifically. Love one person at a time and love that person in specific ways. We become bogged down when we try to love everybody instead of taking on a few as our particular mission. Love in terms of meaning to the other person. Give what is wanted, not what you enjoy giving. Does the person you are trying to love want the kind of help you find so satisfying to provide? What must you do to convey unmistakably to that person that you love and care for him?
- Ask for help. Be willing to receive from other people. Jesus asked people for food, water, help, companionship. When we ask for help, we begin to help others identify and utilize their spiritual gifts. This leads to a healthy Christian body.
- Share decision making. We honor people when we let them in on planning. Include group members in setting goals and determining

strategy. Without shared decision making, group ownership may never develop.

- Pray for group members. Jesus prayed for the disciples. Keep a record of individual needs and then pray for the group as a whole.

Develop Skills of Group Leadership

The small group leader need not be a formal leader in the church (pastor, elder, etc.). Each leader should, however, complete a sixteen-week training course led by the pastor or his trained leaders. As the small group progresses, this leader will adapt more and more to the role of a convener and facilitator.

Actual leadership of the meetings should be rotated within the group from week to week. This enables each group member to fill the role of both follower and leader, thereby preventing one person from dominating and drawing out those who normally would not volunteer to lead. It helps as well if the group has a chronic complainer who is always asking for the group to be conducted in a certain way; when it is his turn to lead, he can do it the way he wants (assuming he has the consensus of the group). No one should be forced into leading, but if the group is accepting and loving, most people will find they will enjoy leading.

The degree of interest and participation is also increased through rotated leadership. It keeps the group from getting into a rut as people from different backgrounds with different insights bring added enrichment.

With rotated leadership, learning is enhanced. The person who leads learns the most. One person's insight sharpens others' understanding of an idea. "As iron sharpens iron, so one man sharpens another" (Prov. 27:17).

Lead by Asking Questions

Every leader should remember that the group meetings must not be a lecture series; they should be informal discussions. The leader's job is to ask the questions and let others do the answering. In the case of a Bible study, this will help the group members to discover for themselves what the Bible says. It is all right if there is silence after a question is asked; this gives people time to think. If the silence becomes awkward, the leader may reword or repeat the question. Learning to ask the right kind of questions is essential in leading a small group (see p. 157).

Lead by Maintaining a Flexible Agenda

Each leader should prepare an agenda and have it accepted by the group through consensus. One common problem for a new leader is that he may become so intent on following his agenda that he will squelch honest, open sharing in order to complete the agenda. The Holy Spirit, however, does not always follow our agenda. Often in the middle of a study a group member may begin to pour out his heart. He may be desperate to be heard. The leader must be sensitive to these divine interruptions, set aside the agenda, and lead the group to minister to the aching heart. A broken heart is so often a teachable heart. *Leaders! Don't miss these opportunities to disciple.* Your bondage must be to the Holy Spirit and not to the agenda.

Lead by Encouraging Participation

Everyone in the group should feel free to participate in various ways. If they are studying a Bible passage, they should feel free to say, "I don't understand this" or "I don't agree with you" or "This is something I've always wondered about." The prepared leader must restrain himself from becoming the answer man. Encourage the group members to answer each other's questions by saying, "What do the rest of you think?"

Make Your Room Setup Work for You

Seating Arrangement

The leader must pay attention to the seating arrangement of the group. The circular arrangement is best so that each group member can have eye contact with every other member and can verbally interact. A common mistake is to put more than two people on a couch, which prevents interaction between those on either end. In most situations, never allow more than two on a couch. Ensure that each person has eye contact with every other person.

Temperature and Lighting

The leader should ensure that the temperature of the room is comfortable and that lighting is adequate. We encourage the host to make the room as light as possible so that body language and facial expressions can be seen.

Two Tools for Good Processing

You may wish to periodically process the group interaction. Processing is a means of determining who in the group is performing what functions and of determining the degree of interaction between the group members. Processing is a good way to help train future small group leaders. However, it is not something that would normally be done in every setting.

Two tools are helpful for good processing:

The Process Diagram

Place the group members' names in a circular pattern on paper in the order in which they are sitting (see fig. 16). Each time a person speaks, draw a line from her name to the person she addressed or to the center of the circle if she addresses the group. Each additional time she speaks in that same direction, place a hatch mark across the line. If one person dominates the conversation, make a hatch mark for every minute he speaks.

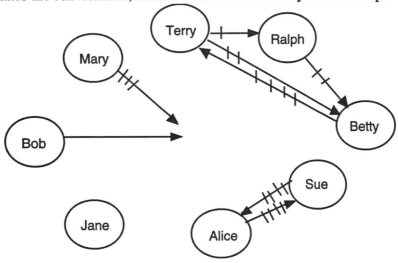

Process Diagram
Figure 16

With this completed diagram, you will be able to determine the quiet and the domineering members of the group. You will also see if anyone has been left out of the interaction and how the members interact with each other. For instance, two talkative people sitting together who talk back and forth with each other (this is a common problem even while other group interaction is taking place) would have an arrow from each to the other with several hatch marks (see fig. 16, Alice and Sue). This problem could gently be mentioned at the end of the meeting, with the hope that the two talkers would avoid that in the future.

Also notice from figure 16, that interaction between the group members is good, with one exception, Jane. She has not spoken, and no one has spoken to her. Someone in the group needs to function as an opinion seeker in order to bring Jane into the interaction. "What do you think about that, Jane?" would draw her in. If the group meeting ends without Jane being drawn in, all but Jane will leave feeling good about the evening. Jane probably will not be back.

The Discussant Function Chart

The processor places the group participants' names in the space provided (see fig. 17). When he observes a participant performing a role function, he simply puts a check in the participant's column, in line with the function he performed. At the end of the meeting, the debriefing of the processor can be helpful to the group and to individuals. Individuals who are performing self-centered functions can gently (humor may help here) be confronted with their behavior. Other members can be encouraged with the roles they performed. This feedback becomes a teaching process. Over a period of time, people become familiar with the functions, and as they perform them, the group interaction will be enhanced.

Four Steps in Building Relationships

At the first few meetings, time should be taken to clarify the purpose of the group, review the norms, build relationships, and take care of housekeeping chores (time and length of meeting, location, refreshments, etc.). Of these items, building relationships must be the main agenda.

During the initial meetings the emphasis should be on building group relationships of love, trust, and acceptance for one another. Sharing is the key to this process. You can't really love and trust one another until you know one another. And you can't know one another until considerable sharing has taken place. This process will probably take approximately three or four two-hour group sessions and perhaps more. This may seem like too much time, but remember that the time is well spent as these relationships will form the foundation for all that follows.

Figure 17
Discussant Function Chart

Date_____ Group_____

Time _____ Observer_____

	Role Functions	Participants' Names							
Group Tasks	1. Idea initiating								
	2. Information seeking								
	3. Information giving								
	4. Opinion seeking								
	5. Opinion giving								
	6. Elaborating								
	7. Coordinating								
	8. Orienting								
	9. Energizing								
	10. Recording								
Maintenance	11. Supporting								
	12. Harmonizing								
	13. Tension relieving								
	14. Gatekeeping								
	15. Norming								
Self-Centered	16. Blocking								
	17. Attacking								
	18. Recognition seeking								
	19. Horseplaying								
	20. Dominating								

A common error of many small groups is to assume that a group can go immediately or too quickly into the study of a book or to the accomplishment of a task without doing the necessary work of building group relationships.

Four steps you may want to follow in building relationships are:

Step 1: History Giving

Ask the group members to tell about themselves in terms of their *past:* where they were born, their family relationships, childhood dreams, outstanding experiences (pleasant and unpleasant), and significant people.

They also should share about their *present:* what exciting things are happening now in their lives.

Finally, they should share something about the *future:* their dreams and goals, where they would like to be in five or ten years, what changes they would desire to take place.

Obviously this sharing process will take time. But this is the most important time in the life of the group. It is the key to knowing and loving one another. It will open the door to mutual ministry and to specific supportive prayer for one another.

Step 2: Affirmation

Spend time telling each group member what you like about him or her and hearing what he or she likes about you. This process brings healing because it helps everyone in the group accept themselves as they are. It is important at this stage that every member be accepted "as is."

Step 3: Goal Setting

Once mutual acceptance and trust are in place, and the group members feel good about each other and themselves, it is time to move on to goal setting. Goal setting begins to focus on deep hurts and areas in which people feel they need to grow. Such areas of sharing might include relationship with spouses, family or peers or perhaps their difficulty in coping with a difficult situation or weakness, such as an inability to handle money or lack of self-control and so on. Personal goals are then set to produce strength and victory in these areas.

This sharing is difficult but fruitful because of the genuine care and concern that has already been developed. The group should be very accepting and willing to spend considerable time in prayer about these goals.

Step 4: Fellowship and Support

Through the presence of the Holy Spirit a unity will develop into a fellowship of strong mutual caring and healing. Prayers will be answered. Testimonies of God's goodness and grace will abound. Jesus Christ will be worshiped and exalted because the group sees firsthand that He is alive and cares. Group members become thankful for one another and sense a genuine holy love for one another. Finally, the plan that Christ has always had for His disciples comes to pass: "By this all men will know that you are my disciples, if you love one another" (John 13:35).

Six Tips for Building Relationships

Tip 1: Touch In

When people arrive, personally greet them and mention personal material from last time. Such greetings might be questions such as "How's your wife?" or "How was your vacation?"

Tip 2: Keep in Touch

During the meeting keep in touch with each member with questions and statements such as "How do you feel about that?" or "I'm interested in your idea concerning that" or "You look bored."

Tip 3: Talk about Problems Now

Don't get lost in the past or the future to the neglect of dealing with what problems group members are having *now*. Encourage people to share their story today.

Tip 4: Stay in Touch with the Person

When somebody makes a personal statement to the group, don't cut it off prematurely. Ask him, "Is that something you'd like to talk about?" Pick up what he has thrown out.

Tip 5: Beware of Labeling

If someone is defensive, don't say, "You are defensive." That is labeling. You may ask "Are you defensive?"

Tip 6: Report Feelings

Be honest enough to report feelings, but don't attack. If you are bored, report "I am bored," but don't report "You bore me." Criticize ideas not persons.

Leading Group Discussions

In leading a small group and motivating people to grow in their Christian walk, you must understand that there are common pitfalls in facilitating discussion on Bible application. We have identified nine ways to maintain good discussion in your small group.

1. Make your questions *conversational.*

2. Use *silence* to your advantage.

3. Be *focused* in your questions.

4. Allow your group to be *spontaneous.*

5. Maintain your sense of *humor.*

6. Limit your *summarizing.*

7. Finish *on time.*

8. Motivate others to *answer questions.*

9. Admit you don't have all the *answers.*

Develop the Skill of Asking Sharing Questions

Sharing questions are questions that encourage people to talk about themselves. For example: "Would you describe a typical day?" "What is the center of warmth in your life right now?" "What would you like people to write on your tombstone?" "What one fruit of the spirit would you like to have and why?" "Where were you born, and would you like to visit that place again?" "What type of work do you do? If you had another choice, would you make it the same?" or "What is your most remembered birthday, and what did you do?"

As the group members share the answers to these and other sharing questions, the group will come to know and understand each other better, which will enhance personal growth.

Never assume that you no longer need to work on relationships. No matter what kind of a small group you have, you must always place a high priority on building interpersonal relationships. Strong personal relationships are foundational to everything else. They form the base and atmosphere for spiritual growth.

A small group can take the form of groups gathered for praying, sharing, worship, Bible study, dialogue, spiritual growth, interests, fellowship, renewal, marriage improvement, singles, parenting, family help, and many more. However, the building of relationships must remain fundamental as discipleship flows out of intimate interpersonal relationships with other believers. You cannot develop to your full potential in Jesus Christ apart from primary interpersonal relationships.

Learn How to Contract and Precontract

Each small group must begin with a contract, either written or unwritten, that clearly defines the purpose for which the small group is meeting and how long it will meet. This contract will help the group to stay on track and avoid confusion among the group participants. (Generally it is not necessary for the average small group in a church to have a written contract. However, clarity of purpose and length of the group's existence is necessary).

A good contract begins with the precontracting process. *Precontracting* refers to the time before the actual small group begins to meet. It is during this time that the purpose of the group is determined and initial participants are recruited.

One precontracting process might work like the following: Two people share a common vision. They work through their vision and clarify what they would like to see happen in a small group. They then talk to two other people, sharing the vision with continual negotiating, until the four people know why the group is going to meet and what will happen in the group. *On this basis* additional people are invited to join the group until there are up to twelve people.

A precontract and contract will include information concerning the type of group to be formed; the length of the initial commitment; the place, day, and time of meeting; basic norms; the number of participants; refreshments; and whether the group will be closed or open. Everyone joining a small group needs to know what he or she is getting involved in. Here is some important information that must be decided on and then shared with prospective small group members:

- Purpose of the group. The "why" precedes the "want to." Clearly explain the big picture of small group life.
- Content of each meeting. Explain the type of Bible study, prayer, worship, and fellowship that you will be enjoying together.
- Location and time of your small group. Make sure they know when, where, and for how long. Open-ended Bible studies will scare many people away.
- Commitment they are agreeing to. Describe the commitment level. Is homework, Scripture memory, or personal sharing expected? It is recommended that the initial commitment for participation should be six to eight weeks. After the initial period is over, the participants may enter again into the same contract or draw up a new contract, depending upon the consensus of the group. At this time, commitments are fulfilled and some participants may wish to drop out, and, depending upon group consensus, new participants may be added. No surprises, please.
- Benefit they will receive. Be positive, not pushy. People must want to be involved. Briefly explain how small groups have impacted your life.

Checklist for Small Group Involvement

1. Did I prepare for the discussion by reading the material carefully and critically?

2. Did I make an effort to get better acquainted with the other members of the group?

3. Did I indicate my interest in the comments of others by listening carefully?

4. Did I look at the person who was talking and make an honest effort to understand his point of view?

5. Did I take an active part in the discussion and offer my comments freely and objectively?

6. Did I relate my comments to those of the previous speaker?

7. Did I keep my comments brief and to the point?

8. Did I share the discussion with others?

9. Did I cooperate in exploring the problem before suggesting possible solutions?

10. Did I concentrate on one phase of the topic at a time and stay with the discussion rather than jumping ahead to other aspects of the topic?

11. Did I make an effort to differentiate between fact and opinion?

12. Did I leave the members with something further to think about?

Ground Rules for Questions

A. Allow people to "pass" if they are not ready to respond. Do check back with them at the end of the sharing time to see if they wish to share. Don't force them to share.

B. Mix questions that call for negative and positive sharing. Don't always ask people to share problems or always to share victories. Mix up the questions.

C. Don't ask follow-up questions after people share unless you intend for only a few to speak. Affirm nonverbally or briefly what has been shared and move to the next person.

D. Ask someone to begin sharing and then go in a circle from there. Begin yourself and be brief, if no one else feels comfortable going first.

E. Watch the time. If the first one or two speak at length, intervene by saying, "Let's share briefly so all may have a chance to speak." Be diplomatic.

F. Never intimidate. If people are struggling with your question, rephrase it. We want our groups to be user-friendly.

CHAPTER SIXTEEN

The Life Cycles of Small Group Ministry

A joke that surfaced about 1992 described "Four Ages of Man": You believe in Santa Claus; You don't believe in Santa Claus; You are Santa Claus; and You look like Santa Claus.

A more serious analysis of the life cycle of mankind includes ten stages of life:

1. Birth

2. Childhood: 0–10 years

3. Preadolescence: 11–12 years

4. Adolescence: 13–18 years

5. Emerging Adults:18–30 years

6. Young Adults: 30–50 years

7. Middle Adults: 50–70 years

8. Senior Adults: 70–80 years

9. Elderly Adults: 80+ year

10. Death[1]

We are familiar, of course, with the basic stages of life: Birth, Growth, Maturity, Decline, and Death (see fig. 18).

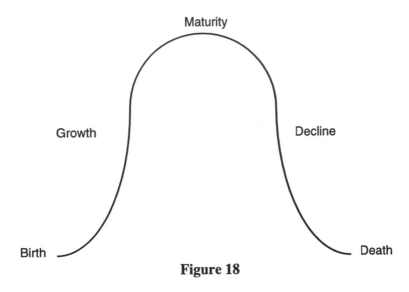

Figure 18

However, we may not be as familiar with the life stages of small groups. In this chapter we will look at two life cycles: the life cycle of group development and the life cycle of group meetings. Both are important for a full understanding of small group ministry in a local church. It is helpful for a small group leader to understand what is occurring at any given time in the life cycle of a group. By understanding the normal sequence of group development, the leader can design the activities of the group to address and resolve the specific issues found at each stage. Thus, the group can develop more smoothly than might normally be the case.

The Life Cycle of Group Development

The small group life cycle is often referred to as "Stages of Group Development."

The Dream Stage

Every small group begins with a person or individuals who have the dream to start a small group. The Dream Stage involves three aspects. First, someone must have a dream to begin a small group. Second, the dream must be shared with others with as much detail as possible at this early stage. Third, initial commitment to at least meet once to discuss the possibility must be secured. Technically this is usually referred to as the "precontract" stage, that is, no commitment beyond initial interest has been secured. We are just in the "idea" or "dream" stage. This stage is crucial to the successful beginning of a small group. If initial excitement and interest is not developed, it is likely that the small group will never come into being.

The Decision Stage

This stage takes place at the very first meeting of the small group. At this meeting, ideas are shared, full discussion takes place, and a final decision is made on whether to begin a small group or not. Key elements of the small group are determined in this first meeting; for example, the time and place to meet, the norms of the group, the type and style of group, the purpose of the group, and how leadership will function. In the technical language of small group development, this is called the "contract" or "covenant" stage. During the first meeting a contract is agreed upon that will govern the small group in its future meetings.

The Delegation Stage

In every group, members take on particular roles or functions. Some will lead the group and others will host it. Someone becomes the time-keeper, always reminding the group when it is time to move on or close for the evening. Another person will serve the group by synthesizing the group's discussion into an acceptable consensus. Group members take on positive roles and negative roles (see following page). Each group member comes to the group with individual expectations and personal agendas. A few individuals may be expecting a great deal of Bible study, while others may want more singing.

It is during this Delegation Stage that individual roles, functions, expectations, and agendas are sorted out. Some small group leaders refer to this period of time as "power and control" since many issues must be determined before the group can become cohesive and bond together. This period of time is not necessarily an angry time but more of a shaking down of ideas, expectations, and procedures. It is similar to a newly married couple who may have a few disagreements during the first year or two of mar-

Positive Roles v. Negative Roles

Positive Roles		Negative Roles	
Proposer:	Initiates ideas and keeps things moving	Onlooker	Is a silent spectator who just nods, smiles, or frowns
Encourager	Involves others and gives approval	Monopolizer	Talks too much, never allowing others to speak
Clarifier	Defines problems and points out issues	Belittler	Takes the dim view and minimizes others
Analyzer	Thinks through and examines issues	Wisecracker	Is indifferent to topic and makes clever remarks
Explorer	Is never satisfied and probes new ideas	Manipulator	Has a hidden agenda and seeks control of group
Mediator	Facilitates harmony and finds the middle ground	Hitchhiker	Jumps on bandwagon and is unwilling to commit
Synthesizer	Puts the pieces together	Pleader	Shares burdens often and always has a cause
Programmer	Is an organizer who points out the ways and means	Sulker	Is a moody person who feels like a martyr

riage but eventually bond together in a common commitment and direction for life. The Delegation Stage is a period of conflict that, if handled well, will lead to a cohesive group. Yet, if the group never is able to reach a common understanding of roles and goals, then the group may never bond together. If a group continues to lack a sense of togetherness or bonding beyond four or five meetings, it is likely that the Delegation Stage has not been resolved. A group leader should be sensitive to the lack of cohesiveness and should schedule the next meeting of the small group to openly discuss the feelings of the group.

The Dedication Stage

At this stage a small group reaches the point where the members bond together. There will be a sense of harmony and cohesiveness among group members. The resistance felt during the Delegation Stage will be gone. Group procedures are agreed upon, roles are defined, and personal opinions are openly expressed. During the Dedication Stage, decisions are made with the full cooperation of all members. Group energy is focused on fulfilling the goals of the group. Problems are solved, and tasks are performed efficiently. This is the most difficult stage for any group to achieve, but it reflects what most people want in a small group experience.

The depth of sharing and cooperation will naturally fluctuate during the Dedication Stage. At times there will be heavy discussions in which members share very personal feelings and experiences. At other times there will be more shallow talk and joking. No group can function continually on an emotional high or in the depths of serious discussion. There must be times of emotional rest during periods of emotional depth. Yet, overall, the Dedication Stage is characterized by group members who trust each other enough to laugh and cry together.

The Decline Stage

As in all life cycles, a period of decline is to be expected. Even in the best small groups, the Dedication Stage will normally not last more than twelve to eighteen months before it begins to dissolve. This is a normal process and should not be interpreted as a negative aspect of small group development. Naturally, people joined the group because it met some specific need in their lives. Individuals may have joined to make new friends, learn more about the Bible, or serve others. Throughout the weeks and months, people will experience growth in their personal and spiritual lives. Some may come to feel that their original needs have been met and that they are now ready to move forward. It is also possible that the original group goals may have been accomplished, and the group is looking for a new direction.

New problems in the group are often indicators that the group has entered into the Decline Stage. First, people may begin showing up late for group meetings. Second, if work is to be completed outside of small group meetings, such as a Bible study, people may come to meetings with incomplete work. Third, an increase in conflict between group members may occur. It may actually feel like the group has reverted to the Delegation Stage (see above). If so, it is likely a signal that the group has entered the Decline Stage. At this point the wise small group leader will call for a meeting to discuss the life cycle of the small group. The entire group should face the situation and decide if they desire to or even can continue on together in the same manner.

The Dead-End Stage

The small group enters this stage when the members decide they cannot continue together without some changes. They have literally reached a dead end and must make some decisions about the future. In some cases a small group may continue to meet and function with ever increasing difficulty. The group is actually at a dead end but just hasn't admitted it. This occurs when a group has bonded closely together and experienced a very supportive Dedication Stage. Each member knows in his heart that the group as it now functions has run its course, but each is unwilling to face this fact publicly. The love and support they feel for one another is so strong that they hate to think of parting.

The Determination Stage

Three possibilities exist for a group that enters this stage. First, the group might decide to develop a new dream; that is, set new goals or begin a new type of group. In this situation the group members often continue to meet, but the direction of the group is changed. A few members may decide not to continue meeting, and a few new members may be invited to join. Essentially the group forms a new dream and begins a new life cycle.

Second, the group might decide to multiply and form two or three different small groups. People's needs and the speed of personal growth vary from one person to another. Groups that functioned well should see the personal growth of each member as an indication of its success. Like having a baby is the normal outgrowth of a couple's expression of love, the multiplying of one or two new groups is an expression of the success of the group.

Third, the group might decide to disband. If this is the decision, it is important that the group meet for one last time to "wrap things up." Don't ever disband without taking the time to bring a sense of closure to the group. After spending time together, it is wise to have a final meeting to allow members to express their appreciation and love to each other.

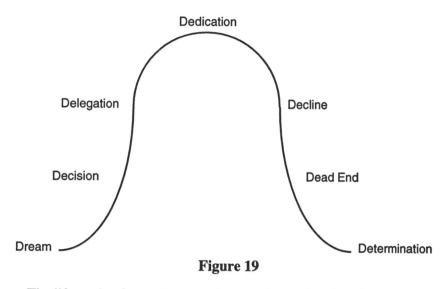

Figure 19

The life cycle of a small group does not imply that there is a clear transition from one stage to another. It should be noted that (1) It is often as difficult to pinpoint the movement from one stage to another as it is to know when a boy becomes a man or a girl becomes a woman. (2) A group may be in one stage while continuing to demonstrate aspects of stages before and after the present stage. (3) Deriving full benefit from each stage is dependent on dealing with the preceding ones. (4) Groups vary in the speed by which they move through the stages. (5) Groups meeting a limited number of times will take longer to move through the stages, that is, a group meeting once a month will take longer to develop than one meeting once a week. (6) The simpler the task of a group, the easier it will be to move through each stage.

The Life Cycle of Group Meetings

Equally important to a small group leader is understanding the normal life cycle of an actual group meeting. Many small groups meet in the evenings after people have arrived home from work or other activities during the day. It is understandable that people arrive at the small group meeting with a low energy level.

During the *Arrival and Opening Phase,* it is appropriate to allow people time to relax, to talk about the day's activities, and generally to acclimate themselves to the meeting. Do not schedule any major discussions or studies during the Arrival and Opening Phase since people are not prepared to undertake such pursuits. Instead, plan your schedule so that it will gradually take group members from one discussion to another as their energy level rises.

Activity Phases 1, 2, and 3 are the major parts of the group's time together. These activities may include a time of singing, a time of prayer, a time of discussion, a time of Bible study, or other activities that the group has determined to be a key part of their time together. In a majority of situations, the group will only have the energy to complete three major activities in a period of one to two hours. Notice how the diagram traces the rise and fall of energy as the small group meeting unfolds (see fig. 20). Once people have settled in, their energy naturally rises and then begins to decline. A small group leader should carefully plan out the evening so that the most important work takes place at the midpoint of the group's time together. Unfortunately, as those who have served on committees can attest, many decisions are placed at the end of meetings, when people are most tired. It is wiser to plan the evening so that times of serious discussion, decision, and confrontation take place more toward the middle of the meeting.

The last phase is the *Conclusion and Departure Phase.* The small group schedule should include a way to assist members to transition out of the meeting and into their homes and lives. In some groups this may mean praying for specific needs each member will face during the coming week. It may mean singing a few closing songs or giving specific assignments or applications from the discussions. Note that once the meeting is officially over, there is again a natural rise in energy level. Refreshments served following a meeting will demonstrate this renewed energy. Or, finding members standing in the parking lot talking for an additional hour following the close of the meeting is another example of how this energy level rises. This is a natural part of the meeting life cycle and should not be resisted but used to continue the application of the Bible study or discussions that were begun earlier in the meeting.

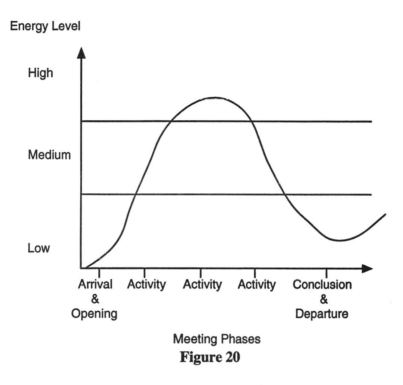

Energy Level

High

Medium

Low

Arrival & Opening   Activity   Activity   Activity   Conclusion & Departure

Meeting Phases

Figure 20

Some Final Thoughts

1. Love *your people*.

How?
- Fall in love *with Jesus*.
- "Jesus replied: 'Love the Lord your God with all your heart and with all your soul and with all your mind.'" (Matt. 22:37)
- The great *commandment* comes before the great *commission*.
- Pray to see your group *through Jesus' eyes*.
- Jesus went through all the towns and villages, teaching in their synagogues, preaching the good news of the kingdom and healing every disease and sickness. When He saw the crowds, He had compassion on them, because they were harassed and helpless, like sheep without a shepherd. (Matt. 9:35–36)
- Pray for your group *by name*.

2. Be tuned up *spiritually*.

How?

• Maintain regular *Bible study and reading*.

Do your best to present yourself to God as one approved, a workman who does not need to be ashamed and who correctly handles the word of truth. (2 Tim. 2:15)

• Maintain regular *prayer time*.

3. Encourage *participation*.

How?
- Remember you are a *facilitator*.
- Keep people in a *circle*.
- *Delegate* areas of responsibility.
- Encourage *teamwork*.

4. *Enjoy your group*.

How?
- Be *prepared*.
- Be *open-minded*.
- Let God *lead*.
- Focus on the *positive*.
- Be *honest with yourself*.
- Remember, it's *God's group*.

5. *Follow up* during the week.

How?
- Personal *notes*.
- Phone *calls*.
- *Pray* for the requests.

6. Handle people's problems *one-by-one*.

How?
- *Love* them.
- *Talk* to the Small Group Pastor.
- *Confront* them privately.

7. Keep *growing*.

How?

- By attending a leadership meeting at least quarterly. Give it a name such as S.A.L.T. : Shepherds Advanced Leadership Training.

Notes

Chapter 1

1. Carl F. George, *How to Break Growth Barriers* (Grand Rapids, Mich.: Baker Book House, 1993), 186.

2. Chuck Colson, *The Body* (Dallas: Word Publishing, 1993), 285.

3. Douglas L. Fagerstrom and James W. Carlson, *The Lonely Pew* (Grand Rapids, Mich.: Baker Book House, 1993), 13.

4. Robert Banks, *Paul's Idea of Community* (Grand Rapids, Mich.: Eerdmans, 1980), 13.

5. See Matthew 28:19–20.

6. Margaret L. Usdansky, "Baby Boomers Hit the Brakes after Life in the Fast Lane," *USA Today*, 24 June 1993, 11A.

7. *Answers to Your Mental Health Questions* (Arlington, Va.: National Mental Health Association, about 1996), 4–10.

8. Gary McIntosh and Glen Martin, *Finding Them, Keeping Them* (Nashville: Broadman & Holman, 1992).

9. James W. Moore, "Is There Life after Stress?" (Nashville: Dimensions for Living, 1992), 63.

Chapter 2

1. Thomas H. Troeger, *The Parable of the Ten Preachers* (Nashville: Abingdon Press, 1992), 20–22.

2. "Quotes and Comments," *The United Church Observer* (September 1992): 48.

Chapter 3

1. Portions of this chapter were previously published in Rodney J. Dean and Gary L. McIntosh, *How to Start or Evaluate a Small Group Ministry* (Lynchburg: Church Growth Institute, 1991). Used by permission.

2. Reported by Bob Conklin in *Daily Development* (Minneapolis, Minn.), nd.

3. "The Goose Story" is available on video from Training Resource Center, Eastern Kentucky University, 217 Perkins Bldg., Richmond, KY 40475, (606) 622–1497.

Chapter 4

1. See the authors' book, *Finding Them, Keeping Them*, 76–86.

2. Adapted from Kevin M. Thompson, *Equipping the Saints: A Manual for Small Group Ministry*, (Minneapolis: Christians in Action Campus Ministry, 1981).

Chapter 5

1. Dr. George B. Wirth gave this illustration to The Seven World Corporation, P.O. Box 11565, Knoxville, TN 37939. It was quoted in "FebBonus," of the Jan/Feb/Mar *Dynamic Preaching*.

2. Gary L. McIntosh and Glen S. Martin, *The Issachar Factor: Understanding Trends That Confront Your Church and Designing a Strategy for Success* (Nashville: Broadman & Holman, 1994), 11–12.

Chapter 6

1. Roy Robertson, *The Road to Discipleship* (Singapore: NavPress, 1992), 40–41.

2. For an overview of the builder, boomer, and buster generations see Gary L. McIntosh, *Three Generations: Riding the Waves of Change in Your Church* (Grand Rapids, Mich.: Revell, 1995).

3. Ibid., 66–68.

4. Glen Martin and Dian Ginter, *Drawing Closer: A Step by Step Guide to Intimacy with God* (Nashville: Broadman & Holman, 1995).

5. For more information on this strategy, call 1-800-295-3787.

Chapter 7

1. Billy D. Strayhorn, *Parables, Inc.* (Platteville, Colo.: Saratoga Press), June 1991: 7.

2. George Barna, *The Power of Vision* (Regal Books: Ventura, Calif., 1992), 28.

3. For further insights on church values see Gary L. McIntosh, *The Exodus Principle* (Nashville: Broadman & Holman, 1995), 15–29.

4. Bill Hybels, "Up to the Challenge," *Leadership* (Fall 1996), 59–60.

Chapter 9

1. Craig Brian Larson, *Illustrations for Preaching and Teaching* (Grand Rapids: Baker, 1993), 128.

2. Martin and Ginter, *Drawing Closer*.

3. Larson, *Illustrations*, 26.

Chapter 10

1. The Slow Track Model is based on the model-group method described by Roberta Hestenes in *Building Christian Community through Small Groups* (audiocassette package). Order from Fuller Theological Seminary Bookstore, Pasadena, CA 91182.

2. For a more detailed manual on using the Slow Track Model see Dr. Rodney J. Dean and Dr. Gary L. McIntosh, *How to Start or Evaluate a Small Group Ministry* (Lynchburg, Va.: Church Growth Institute, 1991).

Chapter 12

1. From *The Song of the Bird*, by Anthony de Mello. Submitted by Wilfred Webb Jr., "Pastor's Story File," May 1992, 3.

2. Donald T. Phillips, *Lincoln on Leadership* (New York: Werner Books, 1992), 68–69.

3. James Burns, *Revivals, Their Laws and Leaders* (London: Hodder & Stoughton, 1909), 95, as quoted in J. Oswald Sanders, *Spiritual Leadership* (Chicago: Moody Press, 1967), 37–38.

Chapter 14

1. Ric Lehman, "Don't Believe the Lie!" *Equipping the Saints* (Winter 1994): 8–9.

2. Ibid., 9–10.

Chapter 15

1. Source Unknown.

Chapter 16

1. Win Arn, "A New Paradigm for Ministry: Middle Adults," *L.I.F.E. LINE*, 3, nd.

Bibliography for Further Study

Coleman, Lyman. *Small Group Training Manual.* Littleton, Colo.: Serendipity House, 1991.

George, Carl. *Prepare Your Church for the Future.* Tarrytown, N.Y.: Revell, 1991.

Gorman, Julie. *A Training Manual for Small Group Leaers.* Wheaton, Ill.: Victor Press, 1991.

Hamlin, Judy. *The Small Group Leaders Training Course. Teachers Manual.* Colorado Springs: NavPress, 1990.

Hestense, Roberta. *Building Christian Community Through Small Groups.* Pasadena, Calif.: Fuller Seminary, 1985

McIntosh, Gary and Rodney Dean. *How to Start or Evaluate Your Small Group Ministry.* Forrest, Va.: Church Growth Institue, 1991.

Meier, Paul, et al. *Filling the Holes in Our Souls: Caring Groups that Build Lasting Relationships.* Chicago: Moody Press, 1992.

Neighbour, Ralph. *Where Do We Go from Here? A Guide for the Cell Group Church.* Houston, Tex.: Touch Publications, 1990.

Resources for Further Study

- *Cell Church Magazine.* This is a quarterly publication that focuses on growing a successful small group minstry. Articles include subjects such as prayer, evangelism, leadership training, etc. Call 1-800-735-5865 to subscribe. Cost: $12.00 per year
- New Hope Community Church, Portland, Oregon. This church is a leader in small group ministry. Call 1-800-935-HOPE for information and order form.
- *Discipleship Journal.* A bi-monthly magazine for anyone serious about small groups and discipling believers. To subscribe write to:

    Discipleship Journal Subscriptions
    PO BOX 54470
    Boulder, CO 80322-4470

- *The Church Growth Network.* A monthly newsletter which creatively summarizes information for leaders. Permission is granted for unlimited use in your own church. Subscription cost is $15.00 per year. To subscribe write to:

    The Church Growth Network Newsletter
    3630 Camellia Dr.
    San Bernardino, CA 92404

- *LEADERSHIP.* A practical journal for church leaders containing full length articles on various ministry topics. Call 1-800-777-3136